THE OLD ENGLISH SHEEPDOG

MRS. KEELING has been breeding and rearing Old English Sheepdogs for many years and she here writes for all admirers of the breed, whether they wish to buy one as a pet or whether they wish to take up serious breeding themselves.

Included in this handbook are chapters on the history of the breed, the breed's standard, general management, breeding, whelping and puppy rearing, showing, and common ailments, together with a list of specialist kennels breeding Old English Sheepdogs, and details of breed clubs.

THE OLD ENGLISH SHEEPDOG

BY
JILL A. KEELING

ARCO PUBLISHING COMPANY, INC.
NEW YORK

Published in the United States of America 1976 by
Arco Publishing Company, Inc.
219 Park Avenue South, New York, N.Y. 10003

Library of Congress Cataloguing in Publication Data

Keeling, Jill Annette.
The old English sheepdog.

(Arco/Foyles pet handbooks)
Bibliography: p.
Includes index.
1. Old English sheepdog. I. Title.
SF429.04K43 1976 636.7′3 76–9848
ISBN 0–668–03973–6

PRINTED IN GREAT BRITAIN

CONTENTS

LIST OF ILLUSTRATIONS

TO MOLLY

(*Bridewell Ladies Model*)

Whose unswerving devotion,

loyalty, companionship, and gentility

have won for all Bobtails

a special place in

my heart

ACKNOWLEDGEMENTS

In the compilation of this book I have been led to approach a diversity of people for information of all kinds, and my thanks are due for the kind co-operation of Mr. F. Brocklesby, Mrs. E. Goodwin, and Mrs. E. Greatorex, who so painstakingly leafed through ancient pedigrees and Show catalogues on my behalf, as well as entrusting me with treasured photographs to provide many of the illustrations. I also owe a debt of gratitude to my sister-in-law, Miss V. Keeling, for the line drawings, and especially to my own veterinary surgeon who so patiently burnt the midnight oil with me in my quest for knowledge before embarking upon the final chapter. Last, but not least, I should like to voice my deep appreciation of my husband's noble efforts to relieve me of household duties while I wrote; his criticisms, too, if not always warmly received at the time, have proved invaluable.

J.A.K.

CHAPTER 1

THE DROVER'S BOB-TAILED COLLIE

Nature who made you rough and grey and meek,
Reft you of dogdom's silent power to speak,
Cut off your tribal customary flag,
And left you with nothing you could wave or wag.
Yet, still unfair herself, she made you fair,
A bob-tailed beauty in a mass of hair,
With two dark eyes on which her mind she spent
To make them tender, wise, and eloquent.

ROSEMARY MEYNELL

'This is a shaggy-coated, hard-haired, hard-headed, rough-and-right sort of a dog without much of a tail, very often to be seen accompanying the drovers of the Southern Counties. I have seen some of them, not pretty only, but particularly beautiful, and seemingly possessed of a high degree of intelligence. I dare say if they were as much admired as the Highland Collie they would become refined in their manners, but refinement isn't a strong point with the Bob-tailed Collie, any more that it is with his master. The colour is usually black and tan or steel grey. I like the latter very much; I don't know why, but it strikes me as being a hardier colour.'

Thus writes Dr. Gorden Stables, R.N., in *Our Friend the Dog,* a book published towards the end of the last century, wherein he claims to set forth the show points, properties, uses, peculiarities, etc., and all that is known about every breed. As the paragraph quoted represents all that he has to say concerning the Old English Sheepdog, it seems that already at that early date the origins of the breed were shrouded in mystery, as, indeed, they still are today. Some authorities claim that the Bobtail is by no means an old breed, having been known for only some two hundred years or so, while others believe it to be among the oldest of our English breeds, with its roots shrouded in the veils of antiquity. Unlike the Dachshund or Greyhound, which can be traced back for literally thousands of years, the 'Drover's Bob-tailed Collie' has apparently either been taken so much as a matter of course down the ages that specific mention of it has escaped the records, or else it has been evolved gradually for purely practical purposes by a section of the community who regarded their dogs solely as workers rather than suitable subjects for literary treatises—if, indeed, they were capable of such! Personally I tend towards the view that the Bobtail is a very old type of dog, for his form has changed virtually not at all over the past seventy years, which would hardly be the case were he representing a comparatively young breed which might still be expected to be in a state of transition.

Originally known as the Smithfield, Cotswold Sheepdog, or Cur, the Old English Sheepdog was formerly more of a cattle dog than anything else, and much used by drovers taking cows, sheep or New Forest ponies to Smithfield market; in view of this it seems only reasonable to suppose that he made his debut in the Southern Counties of England, which are indeed, still his main stronghold, although he may also be found in small numbers today from Land's End to John o' Groats. Sheepdogs of similar physical type are to be found in many other countries, however, such as the Spanish Catalonian Sheepdog, the Hungarian Komondor, the Egyptian Sheepdog, and the Italian Maremma, although the latter is perhaps more like a Pyrenean Mountain Dog and is said by some to be descended from the Polar Bear—a theory, I might add, to which I do *not* subscribe! The Russian Owtcharka, too, bears some similarity to our Bobtail, and has even been cited by some authorities as his possible ancestor together with the French Briard, but this seems to me questionable to say the least as the Russian dog is the largest of the European pastoral breeds, being anything up to thirty-two inches in height, and is fawn or tan in colouration. Also communication between our own country and Russia has never been very close and no importation of these dogs from this part of the world has been recorded. On the whole it seems to me logical to suppose that shepherds all over the world reached independently the same conclusion that the best guardian for their flocks would be a dog large and strong enough to keep wolves and other marauders at bay, while at the same time himself resembling a sheep sufficiently in general outline to be a comforting rather than terrifying spectacle to his charges. This does not, of course, cover such breeds as the Alsatian or Collie which have also fulfilled the same functions, but by far the majority of Sheepdogs in every land are by no means dissimilar to our familiar Bobtail, and by their very numbers lend weight to the theory.

In the show ring, Bobtails were very early placed among the exhibits, for dog shows were first firmly established in 1861 and the breed was exhibited at Birmingham in 1873, while the first Old English Sheepdog Club was founded, and a scale of points for the breed laid down, in 1888; the Standard evolved at that date, incidentally, still holds good today, for it has never been altered. Bobtails were regularly being shown all over the country well before the turn of the century, when Challenge Certificates were already offered to them, and one early Champion, Fairweather by name, may still be seen mounted in the Natural History Museum at South Kensington.* She does not now look very imposing by present-day standards, but I daresay the moths have done much to reduce her coat from its former glory! In the beginning, of course, creams and browns were often found among thoroughbred Sheepdogs, but the inauguration of the Standard at once rendered these undesirable, and such colours have now been virtually bred out. While on the subject of Showing, it is interesting to note that the world record for any breed is held by Mrs. Backs of Holland who bred no less than seven Champions in one litter from Champion Perrywood Blue Bonnet and Champion Shepton Grey Idol; the previous record, oddly enough, was also held by a litter of Bobtails bred by Mrs. Shanks of the Pickhurst Kennels, who made up five Champions, Rag Tag of Pickhurst, Lady Flirt of Pickhurst, Pride of Pickhurst, Saucy Girl of Pickhurst, and Dolly Dimple of Pickhurst from puppies out of Peggy Ann of Pickhurst by Wadhurst Bobby of Pastorale.

Although in these days of flats and small semi-detached

* Since this was written, Champion Fairweather has been removed to storage in the Rothschilde's Museum at Tring.

houses, the Old English Sheepdog is by no means the popular pet which he might otherwise be, much is still to be said in his favour in this direction, for his temperament is second to none for sweetness and reliability, while, in spite of his considerable bulk, he is not a dog who is apt to be always under one's feet or clumsy in his movements. One of the few ways in which he has changed during recent years, and probably not for the better, is in this controversial matter of size, for I have it on good authority that a hamper which was large enough to contain a Champion in 1929 would today be barely adequate for a half-grown puppy, and I cannot help feeling that a great deal of harm will be done to what might otherwise be a very popular breed if this marked increase in size continues.

Leaving size apart, however, the Bobtail makes the ideal country pet; I stress 'country' because he is, of course, essentially a pastoral breed and very much out of his element in the concrete wastes of a town or city. His bulk and even temper make him the perfect companion for children, for they cannot readily hurt *him*, while his innate herding instincts lead him to guard *them* faithfully. I have often seen my own children literally bouncing up and down on the back of one of my patient Sheepdogs, who will probably simply walk away with a grunt when he grows tired of the 'game', while a smaller dog will very often snap even if his whiskers are tweaked! Although the massive coat of these dogs may prove a deterrent to some who are wavering on the brink of buying one, my section on grooming will show that this need not entail a great deal of trouble, and I have found that a Bobtail kept in country surroundings generally keeps himself immaculately clean, although I must admit that his town cousins tend to look somewhat grubby about the white parts; his plentiful 'fleece' may, indeed, prove an additional asset, for the combings can be collected and spun into an excellent yarn suitable for either knitting or hand-weaving. If you think that his big feet will bring in a lot of mud in wet weather, remember that you own are still bigger, and a quick wipe with a piece of cloth or an old wash leather as the dog enters the house will easily solve that particular problem. In any event, I am very certain that if you do decide to invest in a Bobtail, his companionship, gentleness, docility, and intelligence will so endear him to you that your next dog will undoubtedly be 'the same again, please!'

CHAPTER 2

THE PERFECT SHEEPDOG

God put hair over the Sheepdog's eyes so that he could not see the faults of those he loved.

Actually, of course, the perfect dog is yet to be born; and who, you may well ask, is to decide what constitutes perfection in any case? Obviously, left to their own devices, no two people would have identical views on this subject, so, in order to bring some degree of uniformity into the realm of dog breeding, the Kennel Club has laid down a 'Standard' for each breed, defining as rigidly as possible those qualities which should be aimed at, as well as prevalent faults to be avoided. Lest it be thought that in so doing the Kennel Club has sought to enforce only its own opinions, it should perhaps be made clear that these Standards were first compiled with the active co-operation of the breed clubs concerned, and so tend to voice the majority votes of the actual fanciers of those breeds. The following is the Kennel Club Standard for the Old English Sheepdog:

SKULL: Capacious and rather squarely formed, giving plenty of room for brain power. The parts over the eyes should be well arched and the whole well covered with hair.
JAW: Fairly long, strong, square and truncated. The stop should be well defined to avoid a Deerhound face. The attention of judges is particularly called to the above properties, as a long narrow head is a deformity.
EYES: Dark or wall eyes are to be preferred.
NOSE: Always black, large, and capacious.
TEETH: Strong and large, evenly placed and level in position.
EARS: Small, and carried flat to the side of the head, coated moderately with hair.
LEGS: The forelegs should be dead straight, with plenty of bone,

removing the body a medium height from the ground without approaching legginess, well coated all round.

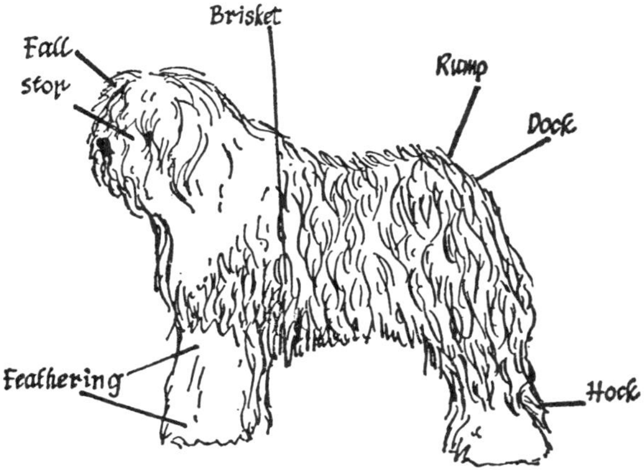

The Points of the Old English Sheepdog

FEET: Small, round, toes well arched and pads thick and round.
TAIL: Puppies requiring docking should have the operation performed within a week of birth, preferably within four days.
NECK AND SHOULDERS: The neck should be fairly long, arched gracefully, and well coated with hair, the shoulders sloping and narrow at the points, the dog standing lower at the shoulders than the loin.
BODY: Rather short and very compact, ribs well sprung and brisket deep and capacious. The loin should be very stout and gently arched, whilst the hind quarters should be round and muscular, and with well let down hocks, and the hams densely coated with a thick long jacket in excess of any other parts.
COAT: Profuse and of good hard texture, not straight, but shaggy and free from curl. The undercoat should be a waterproof pile when not removed by grooming or season.
COLOUR: Any shade of grey, grizzle, blue, or blue merle, with or without white markings, or in reverse, any shade of brown

or sable to be considered distinctly objectionable and not to be encouraged.

HEIGHT: Twenty-two inches and upwards for dogs, slightly less for bitches. Type, symmetry, and character of the greatest importance, and on no account to be sacrificed to size alone.

GENERAL APPEARANCE: A strong, compact-looking dog of great symmetry, absolutely free of legginess or weazleness, profusely coated all over, very elastic in its gallop, but in walking or trotting he has a characteristic ambling or pacing movement. His bark should be loud with a peculiar 'pot-casse' ring in it. Taking him all round, he is a thick-set, muscular, able bodied dog, with a most intelligent expression, free of all Poodle or Deerhound character.

There is also laid down for the guidance of judges the following scale of points:

Head	5	Nose	5
Eyes	5	Teeth	5
Colour	10	Legs	10
Ears	5	Neck and Shoulders	10
Body, loin, and hindquarters	20	Coat	15
		Jaw	10

All this may be crystal clear to anybody who already knows a good deal about Bobtails, but to the novice, as is the case with most breed standards, it may easily lead to considerable confusion, as many points are not clarified at all while others are vague in the extreme. At first glance, too, the beginner may think that many of the 'points' have been chosen quite arbitrarily, but closer examination will reveal that virtually all the show points have their origin in the demands made upon the working ancestors of the present day Champions. It will be noted, for instance, that great stress is laid upon intelligence, both in the skull formation and general expression, and anybody who has seen a Sheepdog actually working with sheep will readily understand how vital a factor this is. It is also interesting to observe that, even in dogs which come from a long line of show stock, the herding instinct is still very much in evidence and will come to the fore at every opportunity which offers. One of my own bitches has, in fact, killed two hens, not by catching them with her teeth as a Terrier might, but by inadvertently stepping on them as she tried to shepherd them off the premises! I have also found that my dogs react immediately, intelligently, and correctly to the goats, whenever the two species happen to meet. Similarly the jaw formation is not such as is usually associated with a hunting dog, or one bred for killing, while the strong evenly placed teeth enable their owner to administer a warning nip to the heels of his charges who refuse to go where he is trying to drive them. The generally compact, yet not coarse or heavy, conformation give the animal the strength, speed, and staying power so essential for him in his job, while his loud bark will enable the shepherd to locate him, and so the sheep, in even the foggiest of weather or on the darkest of nights. His dense double coat will keep him warm and dry, although he may have to attend to his charges in all weathers, and even the preference for a wall eye has its origin in the former shepherds' belief that a dog possessing one would never go blind, and is thus a 'working quality', albeit one based in the first place on a fallacy!

Having seen, then, that the breed standard is not something arbitrarily invented by a committee of armchair cynologists, but based on those qualities essential to an efficient Sheepdog, let us look more closely at some of the points and try to see just what they mean, for the novice setting out to choose his very first puppy, would not, I feel, have a very clear picture of the perfect Bobtail in his mind from the standard alone.

The skull should be large, and particularly broad; in a good adult dog the top of the head, from eye to eye, can barely be spanned by a man's hand, while the ideal length for the upper jaw from the black nose to the stop, or point where the forehead starts to rise, is roughly the width of a man's hand without the thumb. One very important characteristic of the head, which is not mentioned in the Standard at all, is the fall, a fringe of long hair which should grow down right over the eyes and may well even conceal most of the nose also! A Sheepdog with no fall would not go far in the Show ring; and, contrary to popular belief, this does not impair the animal's vision, for the hair is held away from the eyes by the long lashes, so that the dog can see through it perfectly, as through a veil. Actually, this feature was originally thought essential for the working dog, as it afforded the eyes protection from the wind and sun, and one school of thought still believes that the removal of the fall is liable to cause blindness, although I do not myself think this to be the case.

Much controversy has arisen over the matter of wall eyes. This term is used to define those cases wherin the eyes are of different colours, most often pale china blue and brown, the unusually coloured one, in this case the blue, being the wall eye. The term is thought to be derived from an old belief that in such cases there was a 'wall' or barrier between the two organs, and should, in my opinion, be used *only* in those instances where there is a marked discrepancy between the pigmentation of the two eyes. Occasionally one sees an Old English Sheepdog with two china blue eyes, when these are often referred to as 'double wall eyes', but this is an obvious misuse of the term, and such dogs should, if one is to interpret the standard strictly according to the letter, be penalized in the show ring as having light eyes. On the other hand, if we remember the original reason for the shepherds' predilection for wall eyes, it is only reasonable to suppose that a 'double wall-eyed' dog would be doubly protected against blindness, so perhaps those judges who do not so penalize them have the meaning if not the letter of the law at heart. Nevertheless, I would not personally class 'double wall-eyes' as a good point but rather the reverse.

Many judges rate a correct mouth very highly, although at least one well known Champion is to my knowledge faulty in this respect. In fact, the 'level in position' specified in the Standard might more accurately read '*very* slightly overshot', for no Sheepdog which I have ever seen has teeth which meet literally edge to edge, but they rather tend to come together in much the same manner as do our own. cases where the teeth are badly either over- or under-shot do, however, also occur, and are both major faults. Unfortunately, the cutting of the adult teeth can often alter a dog's mouth entirely, so that the conformation of the milk teeth in a young puppy is no reliable guide to what they will be like in later years.

One really glaring omission from the Standard, from the point of view of the novice, is that of any definite ruling regarding the tail—or rather, lack of it! Apparently working on the assumption that everybody would know what an Old English Sheepdog should look like, the powers that be did not think fit to specify accurately just where the docking, which they advocated, should take place—is the puppy to be left with a tail like a Fox Terrier, one might well ask, or a Boxer . . .? The answer, of course, is that today no trace of tail at all is left, although in former years the small stump allowed to remain originally gave rise to the now generally accepted nickname of 'Bobtail'. To many, the practice of docking seems barbarous in the extreme, but this custom, in common with many other points specified in the Standard, has its roots in antiquity, when the amputation of a dog's tail was the sign of a shepherd's dog, and carried with it automatic exemption from the payment of a dog licence! It is thought that this practice originated in an attempt to prevent dogs bred for working from straying from their task to chase rabbits and the like, the absence of 'rudder' being a considerable handicap in cornering suddenly when in pursuit of their prey.

On the whole, the remarks in the Standard concerning the general body conformation are too vague to be of much help to the novice, such terms as 'fairly' and 'medium' occurring all too frequently. Here again, however, most of the requirements are conducive to the greater efficiency of the working Sheepdog; a good reach of neck is essential so that a dog ordered to lie down can still observe both his master and his flock above the long grass in which he is most likely to be working, while the 'well let down hocks' (that is, a short last joint to the hind legs, so angulated as to render it almost a continuation of the foot) have the effect of snow shoes when the dog has to work over snow or swampy ground. The sturdy hindquarters, placed higher than the fine shoulders, lend strength and speed to his gallop, and the good bone and lack of legginess add the power necessary to carry so weighty a body for long distances over any type of terrain. Although not mentioned in the Standard, the weight of a Sheepdog standing twenty-two inches at the shoulder might well be ninety pounds or so, while I have known larger specimens who weighed well over a hundredweight, so it is obvious that a very stout frame is essential if the legs are not to buckle beneath the great body! In fact, cow hocks, or, in effect, knock-knees in the hind legs, are all too common in this breed, and tend to give a very bad movement; to cure this failing, every effort should be made to prevent dogs, especially young ones, from rearing up on their hind legs, a habit which probably does more than anything else to bring about this condition.

All these points, of course, apply to the adult dog, and the novice, confronted with a medley of puppies from whom he hopes to choose his first winner, will very likely be completely non-plussed; indeed, few of even the most experienced dog fanciers would claim to be able to choose a good one from the nest with anything like infallibility. One can, however, look for a good eye colour—and this includes a nice dark rim round the eyes, a feature often absent in puppies with white heads but which *may* develop in later life—a sound, sturdy frame, large head, and wholly black nose, although this feature again may develop up to the age of one year or more. Nevertheless, a butterfly nose, or one which is still spotted with the pink of early puppyhood, is best avoided, as it may be a permanency. Small feet, too, are difficult to assess in the immature, but in the adult the front feet should appear only as an unbroken continuation of the straight line of the legs, an effect which is, of course, greatly helped by the 'feathering' or thick and upstanding hair on these limbs. Above all, of course, a healthy and lively puppy should be chosen, for even the best whelp is unlikely to develop into a first-class adult without the good constitution so essential to all top notchers.

Having chosen his puppy, the novice's next meeting with the Standard is likely to be on the occasion of his first essay in the Show ring, and here he may well meet with a rude awakening, for judges, I am afraid, all too often rely on their own acquired knowledge and experience without reference to the laws laid down for their guidance, and, indeed, sometimes appear to have forgotten the Standard altogether. The most glaring example of this is probably the favouring of what is fashionable as against what is correct; for example, at the time of writing blue is in vogue as the most popular colour for an Old English Sheepdog, and I have seen dogs with perfect grey or grizzle coats put down, admittedly for no other reason than that their colour was other than blue, with utter disregard for the fact that it was equally correct. At the same time, many dogs with decidedly *brown* coats often go to the top, in spite of the very definite ruling that such colouration is 'distinctly objectionable and not to be encouraged'! Similarly there is in the Show ring today a definite preference for larger dogs—one of no more than the specified twenty-two inches being more than likely to be put down as too small. Personally, I feel many Bobtails being bred, shown, and made up into Champions today are far *too* large, being too clumsy to make efficient working Sheepdogs, and too bulky to be welcomed as pets in the average home; they look showy and attractive, to be sure, but what is the object of producing showy, attractive animals if they cannot find homes other than among the comparatively slender ranks of show-goers?

CHAPTER 3

GENERAL MANAGEMENT

The dog is the only animal who has seen his god.

ANON.

All too often I have heard so-called dog lovers express the opinion that a dog is no trouble at all as a pet, because one can easily be fed with the scraps from his owners' table, and requires no special attention in other directions. In fact, of course, nothing could be further from the truth, and, while I should be the last person to suggest that looking after a dog is an onerous task, or that the prospective purchaser of a puppy is laying himself open to a future life of hard labour, I do very strongly believe that anybody who is not prepared to feed, house, and otherwise care for a dog in a manner suited to the animal's well being, has no right to keep one at all.

FEEDING

No two dog owners, I suppose, would agree in every particular on the best diet for their charges, but before you come to a final decision on the all-important matter of the menu with which you intend to provide yours, it is only common sense to find out just what his natural requirements are. All animals, of course, require protein (body-building food), carbohydrates (energy-producing foods), and many different minerals, such as iron and calcium if they are to develop and maintain really healthy bodies, but the digestive tracts of the varying groups of animals are adapted to obtain these essentials from different sources. Zoologically speaking, the dog is a carnivore, or flesh-eating animal, and consequently has a short gut capable of deriving most forms of nourishment from the highly concentrated but easily digestible raw meat which, in a wild state, he used to provide for himself by hunting and killing smaller herbivorous or vegetable-eating animals. The contents of the stomach and intestines of such animals would often provide the dog with all he required in the way of carbohydrate and vitamins, while the bones contained calcium and other minerals, so that very little vegetable matter as such was needed to keep him fit and well. As a result his teeth as well as his alimentary canal have taken on a form best suited to the deriving of nourishment from this source. The basis, then, of the domestic dog's diet should unquestionably be raw meat, and, if this were fed complete with bone and offal, it might well constitute the entire menu, provided always that the dog in question had free access to grass and other vegetation from which he could himself select whatever was necessary to make good any deficiencies. The scrap-feeding advocates would do well to remember that we ourselves belong to a different animal group altogether, and a meal of potatoes, bread, and gravy, with only an odd remnant of meat thrown in, is as unsuitable for his dog as one composed entirely of raw meat would be for him!

As most domestic dogs cannot be fed upon whole carcases, and furthermore do not enjoy free access to all types of vegetation, it is incumbent upon their owners to provide them with as near an approximation as possible to their natural diet, and to this end a liberal supply of raw meat is the first essential. Many breeders advocate cooked meat, but as this process undoubtedly destroys much of the vitamin content, besides being, of course, quite unnatural, and providing too little work for the dog's gastric juices, I personally prefer to give a preponderance of raw food unless some unusual reason, such as very hot weather when my supplies will not keep good as long as necessary, intervenes. Similarly, raw vegetables such as carrot or cabbage may with advantage be added to the diet, while a reputable brand of whole-meal dog biscuit or brown bread will supply additional carbohydrate as well as the essential roughage. White bread, incidentally, should never be given, as it is over-refined and the agene content is thought to be definitely harmful. Most dogs seem to do best on one large meal a day, with perhaps a bedtime biscuit during the cold weather, and it is as well to remember that far more harm can be done by overfeeding than by slightly underfeeding; in the natural state a carnivore often has to go hungry, and its constitution is adapted to withstand this, and, indeed, many owners fast their dogs completely one day each week, when the rest to the digestive system is probably more beneficial than otherwise. Personally I do not adopt this procedure—but, I must admit, more out of consideration for myself than for the dogs, as I find their accusing and hungry faces too much for me when I sit down to a hearty dinner myself! Occasionally, however, I do manage to harden my heart, and the dogs seem all the better for my 'starvation' treatment. An occasional drink of milk will also do no harm, although it is best to remember that this substance was designed by nature for the nourishment of the very young only, and too much given to an adult animal tends to cause permanent diarrhoea.

The ideal diet, then, for the adult Sheepdog is at least one pound of raw meat each day, together with rather less brown bread or biscuit soaked in gravy (I find a sheep's or calf's head ideal and cheap for making this without cooking the actual meat), and a sprinkling of grated carrot or cabbage. Many breeders also give some proprietary brand of yeast tablets as a vitamin supplement, but, while the dogs appreciate these as 'sweets', I have not myself noticed any marked effect upon the animals' health from this source. There are also on the market a wealth of garlic, seaweed, and what-have-you tablets, but here again I feel that such should not be necessary provided that the basic diet of raw meat is adequate. Big, meaty marrow bones are excellent for the teeth, and also, I believe, help to stimulate the digestive juices, but cooked bones, especially small ones, tend to splinter and may easily cause serious trouble in the form of a perforated intestine. Chicken and rabbit bones should never be given. A constant supply of clean, fresh water should always be available, and the bowl will need frequent replenishing as the Bobtail is, as are most long-haired animals, a thirsty dog and often a very fussy one if the water available is not just as he thinks it should be. One of my own dogs, in fact, will invariably demand fresh water whenever he goes to the bowl, and, as his method of doing this is to upset the remnants over the kitchen floor with his paw, I find it pays to accede to his request on the first time of asking!

Although we may all be idealists when planning our dog's menu, it is as well to bear in mind that we are also all human, and a variety of reasons can intervene to prevent our plans from coming to fruition. Fortunately for us, the dog is an adaptable creature, and if for some unforeseen reason the meat supply fails, or the new consignment of biscuit does not arrive before the old is finished, no great harm will be done if he has to go on short commons for a day or two; an *occasional* meatless day will not ruin his digestion for ever, and, in an emergency, a visit to the fishmonger will often produce fish scraps or chicken offal which can be stewed up into a most appetizing meal—indeed, the change may well be a welcome one, for do not forget that your dog can get as bored with his meals as you would be if you had roast beef and yorkshire pudding every day of the week. Occasional meals of fish, tripe, chicken offal, or even cheese will go a long way towards keeping his appetite keen and healthy, and, above all, do not make the mistake of attributing your own tastes to your dog and trimming off all the fat and gristle, for both are beneficial to him and will be relished, although *too* fatty a diet, of course, such as breast of lamb, will generally lead to undesirable obesity.

HOUSING

Personally I feel very strongly that the ideal accommodation for any dog is in his master's house, but, obviously, if one keeps a number of large dogs or has unusually cramped quarters oneself, this is not always practicable, and in such cases a spacious and comfortable kennel must be provided. Similarly, litters of young puppies just 'out of nappies' are something of a trial in even the most dog-loving of households, and can best be housed out of doors. For the adult Bobtail the best type of kennel is, in my opinion, of the shed rather than the conventional type, and one seven feet by four feet six inches, and about five feet high would not be too large, particularly if the dog is likely to be confined in it for any considerable periods of time. A large barred window on the same side as the door to avoid unnecessary draughts and, in the case of puppies, low enough to avoid providing the occupants with an urge to stand up and look out, is an essential, and should be furnished with an adjustable shutter which can be lowered in summer and closed in inclement weather or should the animal ever be unwell. This, without any further refinements, is perfectly adequate for the dog who normally has free range of his owner's house and/or garden during the greater part of each day, and may expect to be kennelled only at night, when he will require nothing more in the way of a bed than is afforded by a liberal covering of clean straw on the floor. Those dogs which are unfortunate enough to be kennelled more or less permanently, however, except at their regular exercising times, naturally need more elaborate quarters, and in these cases brick built kennels are undoubtedly the best, affording excellent insulation against all extremes of temperature —in fact, all the advantages of a well built human dwelling. As such kennels usually have concrete floors, it is essential that they be supplied with raised sleeping platforms made from wood, and they are also greatly improved by having an additional outer compartment, roofed over but with two or even three of its sides constructed from chain link netting to give the confined dog at least some semblance of fresh air; a large run would, of course, be even better, although this will entail the owner's keeping his weather eye open for rain as most dogs appear to enjoy lying out in even quite heavy showers, and once their coats become really sodden it is a lengthy business to dry them off again sufficiently to ensure against rheumatism.

Even the house dog should ideally be provided with his own bed in a corner to which he can retire to be out of the family's way, and where he can bury his most treasured bones, or gnaw them without fear of frantic admonitions to 'mind the carpet'! The Bobtail, although large by most people's standards, is by no means a clumsy or bumptious dog, and although his shaggily-clad feet are apt to carry with them quite a noticeable quota of mud or moisture, if well groomed he should not create too much of an upheaval in a normal household, and the joy of his companionship will more than compensate for any mess he *does* make. In any event, but particularly if your dog is one of the less fortunate individuals who is liable to be kennelled for long periods, I do feel that many owners do not fully understand that the dog is by nature a gregarious pack animal for whom there can be no worse fate than *solitary* confinement, so do, if you can possibly manage it, keep more than one dog, and your pet's happiness will then be complete.

EXERCISE

A very great deal has been written on this subject—so much, indeed, that I cannot help feeling that many prospective dog owners have been discouraged from putting their plans into operation through fear of the daily marathons which many writers on this topic would have us believe are essential to the well being of any dog. While, in my experience, every dog thoroughly enjoys a good long walk or a gallop over the fields, for him as for most of us, the normal daily round as he goes about his business—in his case most often that of trailing his master as he goes about *his*!—is quite adequate to keep him in good health. I am fully aware that this statement will almost certainly bring down a storm of invective upon my head from all quarters, but the fact remains that I have at present a round dozen dogs living in and about my house, none of whom, due to unavoidable circumstances, have I the time to exercise regularly, yet all are in the pink of condition, good movers in the Show ring, and bursting with vitality and *joie de vivre* as they romp and play together. Ideally, of course, I, too, think that a good walk at least twice a week is beneficial to any dog, both physically and mentally, and a daily walk even more so, but the novice should not be misled into the belief that his new dog will fade away and die if not made to trudge over five or six miles of hard unyielding road every afternoon, for nothing could be further from the truth, and, if left to his own devices, he will provide himself with quite enough exercise for his immediate needs, thank you! In my view many breeders try to adhere to far too rigid a timetable for their charges' good, for working by rule of thumb is quite contrary to all the laws of nature. A wild carnivore does not obtain precisely the same amount of the same kind of food at the same time each day, or expend exactly the same amount of energy in obtaining it, and his system is not adapted to respond to a strict routine.

Many domestic dogs are afflicted with a condition known zoologically as 'cage-back', where an abnormally arched loin indicates that too regular feeding has given insufficient play to the stomach muscles, which have grown stiff and set in consequence. Similarly many dogs are stiff and awkward in their movements, being allowed far too little freedom to exercise their legs unrestrainedly. So throw routine to the winds; feed your dog at four o'clock today and seven o'clock tomorrow; take him for a ten-mile tramp on Sunday and none at all on Monday if it suits you —he will be all the better for it, and so will you!

GROOMING

To groom, or not to groom, that is the question! As a novice buying my first bitch, I approached many Bobtail owners of long standing on this point, and received such a diversity of replies that I had to choose between being guided by my own common sense and observation, or risking lunacy by endeavouring to follow so many diametrically opposed advisers. The owner of one champion told me that she groomed him 'once in a while', when she had time; while another *combed* hers twice each day. One school of thought claims that too frequent grooming removes the undercoat—fatal if you wish to show your dog; another that only daily brushing will prevent the formation of clots with equally disastrous results. Most advocate the use of the brush rather than the comb, although the owner of one famous champion—but surely this is where we came in!

The truth of the matter, of course, is that it all depends on the dog. Leaving aside the requirement set forth in the Kennel Club Standard that the Old English Sheepdog shall have a harsh coat, there would appear to be two quite different qualities of coat prevalent in the breed—those which clot, and those which do not. As both appear in closely related dogs, such as mother and son, or two litter sisters, it appears to be entirely a matter of luck which type it falls to *your* lot to cope with. Assuming that you keep a dog purely as a pet, one with an easy coat should remain quite comfortable and presentable with only a weekly grooming, or even less, but a really difficult coat will require daily brushing if it is not to coagulate into a thick mat of inseparable wool all

Old English Sheepdog puppies, bred by Mrs. Bushby

Krisma Magic Moments in Jedforest
Junior warrant in 12 months, owner Mrs. J. Collins

over the dog's body. In my opinion, a dog with this type of coat is better clipped annually, if not required for show, unless you can guarantee to spend at least half an hour each day keeping it free from the earliest tendency to clot.

The practice of clipping is, of course, not to be generally recommended, as the profuse coat of the well kept Bobtail constitutes one of his greatest charms, but in certain circumstances it may be desirable or even essential. One of these is in the case of the whelping bitch, when, unless the hair on the chest and abdomen is removed the teats will be inaccessible to the newly born puppies, as well as impossible to keep clean. (See page 48.) Some time, therefore, prior to the happy event—anything from one to three weeks, but preferably before the distension of the abdomen and udders render the task unnecessarily difficult—the hair on these parts should be carefully clipped as short as possible, and I find it also advisable to shorten the hair all over the body, particularly on the legs. Some time after whelping the bitch will cast her coat anyhow, and clipping it to a length of some three or four inches will prevent its being reduced to a tangled mat by the sucking, tugging, and scrabbling of the litter which, even after weaning, will delight in chewing and swinging on their mother's coat if this be left of sufficient length to enable them to do so. Many breeders, of course, prefer to leave the bulk of the coat long and risk the resulting mess, but the clipping of the under parts is absolutely essential, and *must* be undertaken before the puppies can feed, even if it be delayed until during or after the actual birth. Obviously this is by no means ideal, but accidents and oversights can happen in even the best regulated kennels, and I well remember one bitch of mine who produced a perfectly healthy litter a whole week prematurely, thus catching me out properly. In her case, I *had* to clip her between births—with no ill effects, although I was greatly concerned at having to add to her troubles at such a time.

Another occasion when I strongly advocate the clipping of a Bobtail is if the owner realizes that he is unlikely to have time to pay sufficient attention to grooming for any considerable period. It is much better to clip your dog at the beginning of such a period than to wait until the coat has become so matted that no other course is feasible, and clipping only with difficulty. Too many Sheepdogs have been brought to me in this shocking condition for me to be able to advise any other course, and I cannot condemn too strongly the owners who allow this to come about. Anybody can become so busy that daily or even weekly grooming is out of the question, but nobody with any sense of responsibility towards their pet could possibly begrudge the odd hour or so which is all that is necessary to clip him before his coat becomes irreparably clotted. A reasonably well groomed coat can easily be clipped to any length by lifting the coat with either a comb or the fingers of one hand while the scissors are wielded with the other, special attention being paid to that round the base and fringes of the ears, and 'under the arms' where clotting is most likely to occur; the task is quick and easy, and the result not unattractive.

Assuming that you are the proud owner of a first rate dog, it is

Grooming the forequarters

Grooming, rear view

fairly obvious that his coat can make or break him in the Show ring. While *too* long a coat is not desirable (although I knew one bitch whose 'skirts' resembled nothing so much as the trappings of a medieval war horse!) that of the prospective champion must be profuse and liberally endowed with undercoat; the Bobtail in fact, has *two* coats, of which the outer and longer is harsh, coarse, and weather-resistant, while the inner is fleecy, soft and warm. As the combing out of even the smallest clot inevitably also removes its quota of undercoat, it will easily be seen that, unless he has a superlatively easy coat, the Show dog will be all the better for a brushing each day, while the pet, as we have seen, can generally be kept in good trim with a weekly grooming. In either case the same golden rule for procedure applies—*always* start at the bottom and work upwards. By this method the ungroomed hair can easily be held up out of the way of the brush with the left hand, thus ensuring that the portions actually being groomed receive the maximum attention.

We start, then, with the toes of, say, the right hind foot and work up to the rump; then the right fore foot, up to the shoulder, and along the flank to join the groomed hair at the top of the hind leg; and only when all four legs have been thus dealt with should we attend to the back and head. Personally, I find the legs and sides easier to do if the dog can be persuaded to lie down, when the inside of the right legs can be done with the dog in the same position as for the outside of the left legs, and the belly is also easily accessible. So far as possible, the comb should not be used, and, if the animal is kept well groomed, can often be dispensed with altogether except occasionally for toes, elbows, 'under the arms', groin, ears, and beard, and latter sometimes becoming clotted with scraps of food.

In the case of the Show dog, care should be taken to avoid dragging out too much of the undercoat, except on the shoulders where it may be stripped away to enhance the desirable 'pear-shape' of the body as a whole. With the pet animal, of course, the removal of most of the undercoat both here and elsewhere greatly facilitates grooming operations without seriously impairing the appearance of the dog, and is especially to be recommended in hot weather.

Although grooming may generally be described as a pleasurable experience for both the dog and his master, there are a few occasions when this is not the case, for the Bobtail has one unfortunate trait which might well prove an embarrassment to an owner unprepared to deal with it. Possibly owing to his lack of tail, a dog of this breed periodically soils himself when voiding

Grooming the hindquarters

faeces, and, if he appears to have difficulty in passing his motions, the hair round the anus should at once be examined, for, if he has not been groomed for a day or two, it may well be found that a large cake of faeces has been formed in such a position as effectively to prevent the expulsion of any more. Under these circumstances it is best either to stand the dog on a sheet of newspaper or take him out into the garden, and there carefully comb away the offending matter. Should this still be moist, I find it best either to wash the affected area after as much faeces as possible has been removed with the comb, or to leave the remnants to dry for an hour or so and then comb again. Of course, this situation arises only when the dog has some form of diarrhoea and so should not be a frequent occurrence in a healthy animal.

At least once a week the dog's ears should be cleaned thoroughly and examined for canker, an ailment to which, like all long-coated breeds, the Bobtail is particularly susceptible. As a precautionary measure, I find it best to use a twenty-five per cent calamine and spirit lotion (twenty-five per cent calamine and seventy-five per cent spirit) for the cleaning operation, first wiping over the inside of the ear flaps with a piece of cotton wool soaked in the solution, and then probing gently into the ear itself with another piece wrapped round an orange stick or something similar. Great care should be taken during the latter operation as rough treatment may easily cause permanent injury to the delicate mechanism. Another aid to the prevention of canker is the teasing away of the tuft of reddish brown hair which sprouts from the orifice itself; if left, this clots very readily, and is an excellent harbour for dirt and germs.

When the ears have been attended to, the soles of the feet should next be subjected to careful scrutiny to ensure that no clots of hair have formed between the toes, and any which are discovered should be clipped carefully away with a small pair of sharp scissors. In wet weather mud often coagulates with the hair to form such clots, which can cause severe local irritation if not promptly dealt with, and, in bad cases, even prolonged lameness. I remember once hearing a bitch of mine walking along with a peculiar uneven clicking noise, as though she were wearing a high-heeled shoe on one foot; inspection revealed a boiled sweet, discarded by one of the children, firmly affixed to her hairy pad!

The pads themselves should also be examined for cracking, which can be remedied by the rubbing in of vaseline, and the nails may require trimming from time to time if they become overgrown. Plenty of exercise on hard surfaces is to some extent a preventative of this, but is often insufficient to keep them as short as is desirable, when cutting must be resorted to. For this operation a pair of stout clippers are essential,. (ordinary nail scissors will not look at the job!), and great care must be taken to remove only the dead tip of the nail—which is not as difficult as it might appear, for the pink 'quick' is clearly visible through the horny exterior shell.

It will be found frequently necessary to remove the 'sleep' from the corners of the dog's eyes as the long hair can retain this until quite a large knob of the substance has formed, but this is easily remedied. The teeth should also be examined occasionally for the formation of tartar, a brownish deposit which can hasten decay or cause severe inflammation of the gums. Plenty of hard food and raw marrow bones to gnaw go a long way towards preventing this, but where it is discovered the teeth should be scaled or scraped. This may be done at home (a special scaling implement is available at most pet stores), but the novice might be well advised to let his veterinary surgeon perform the task at first so that he could learn the correct technique by watching an expert at work.

Personally, I do not advocate frequent bathing. A well-groomed dog should, bar accidents, keep his coat sufficiently clean without recourse to the tub, and the Bobtail's shaggy mop of hair is not the easiest in the world to dry. Bathing in winter, therefore, might well prove a dangerous practice, resulting in a severe chill or even pneumonia, and should be undertaken only in the direst necessity. From the point of view of the Show dog, too frequent bathing seems to have a tendency to soften the harsh outer coat, while it also encourages matting of the under-coat, although the white parts may well have to be washed in preparation for a big Show date (see page 48). Some breeders advocate monthly bathing to promote growth of coat; others perfume their dogs' bath water! But this is by the way.

When the Bobtail really is due for a shampoo, the only possible place to give it to him is in the family bath. I generally half fill this with tepid water, and then get an assistant to help me lift the dog in; this renders the operation immeasurably easier, as one person can then control each end of the animal, who is otherwise liable to spreadeagle his legs, scrabble wildly for a foothold on the unfamiliar slippery surface, and finally fall right down in the water with dire results. Having got my subject firmly on his feet in the tub, I first attend to his legs; having wet these thoroughly, I take a good handful of some reliable soap powder, and rub it up into a fine lather on the limb in question, working well down into the thick fur so that the skin too is thoroughly cleansed. Water is next poured over the back, which is lathered in turn, and the head and chest are dealt with last, great care being taken to avoid getting soap and/or water into the eyes, ears, and mouth. When the entire dog has been washed, I rinse the thick of the soap away with the water in which he is already standing before taking out the plug, and, as the water runs out I squeeze as much more as possible out of the now sodden coat, while usually also trying to prevent its owner from 'abandoning ship'!

As you may rest assured that he will endeavour to get out of the bath at some stage in the proceedings, it is as well to wear the oldest possible clothes, for you will almost certainly find yourself nearly as wet as the dog before the whole operation is completed. Fresh water (once again tepid) is now run in with the dog still *in situ*, looking by this time something like a bedraggled long-haired Greyhound, and the entire coat is thoroughly rinsed. Personally I find that two or even three rinsing waters are necessary before I am satisfied that all the soap is out, and, when the last canful has been poured over the sufferer, I find it best to drain the bath and 'wring him out', squeezing handfuls of coat between my fingers, before lifting him out onto a clean towel. Immediately you have put the dog down, stand clear—for this is the moment he has been waiting for to drench you with spray from his first tremendous shake—and only when his initial violent convulsions have subsided is it safe to move in with another towel and start to rub him dry. This, needless to say, is a long and thankless task, for the harder you rub the less effect do you appear to make, and eventually the job must be abandoned apparently only half done, and the dog turned into warm, clean quarters to dry off, a process which may well take anything up to half a day. Some authorities advocate combing the coat while still damp, as they say this prevents any tendency to curl. Personally, I have never observed any such tendency—and anyhow you are likely to be fully occupied for the next half hour or so spring-cleaning the bathroom!

CHAPTER 4

BREEDING

If the history of all the dogs who have loved and been loved by the race of man could be written, each history of a dog would resemble all the other histories. It would be a love story.

JAMES DOUGLAS

A whole library could, I suppose, be filled with the tomes which have been written on this subject, and, as with most other doggy topics, the novice would discover them to contain a bewildering diversity of opinion. He might, therefore, be well advised to adhere religiously to one of them, until such time as he had acquired sufficient practical experience of his own to relate the written word more or less accurately to its likely outcome when applied in practice. Obviously, a handbook of this nature does not afford sufficient scope for any detailed discussion of genetics and the laws of Mendelism, so we must restrict ourselves here to a few broad hints to set the beginner on the right path.

In the case of most small domestic animals, such as Rabbits, Cavies, Rats, Mice, etc., the would-be breeder generally commences with the purchase of a breeding pair or trio, that is, one male and one or two females. In the case of the novice dog breeder, however, he would be well advised to invest all that he can afford in a bitch or bitches, for in this as in many other walks of life it pays to buy only the best, and the price of a really good dog is often prohibitive for any but the most elastic purses. A first rate young bitch may well cost anything from twenty guineas upwards, but, if this figure horrifies you, it is as well to remember that you are likely to breed better and thus more valuable puppies from one bitch of impeccable pedigree than from several inferior animals. Spare no pains, therefore, in the choosing of your foundation bitch, and, if you buy her as a puppy, remember that only the best of food, care, and general attention is good enough for her during her early formative months, for an undernourished or otherwise poorly conditioned bitch will never produce sound stock. (*See Chapter on Puppy Rearing.*) On the other hand, of course, you may be eager to start actually breeding Sheepdogs sooner than would be possible if you started your kennel with a very young puppy, in which case you might well consider the purchase of an adult. As I personally do not recommend mating a bitch until her second season, and the average Bobtail does not appear to come into season until she is at least one year old, and at intervals of from seven to nine months thereafter, it will be seen that the purchaser of a puppy has a long time to wait before she is ready for her first litter, so there is something to be said for this latter course, although many people prefer to bring up their dog in their own way from the earliest age possible. Whichever way you choose, the rule of buying only the very best you can afford applies with equal force, and, if adhered to strictly, should ensure that you have both a bitch and puppies to be proud of.

BREEDING TERMS

Occasionally one may see offered for sale a bitch on breeding terms. This may well provide a solution for a would-be breeder who lacks sufficient capital to buy his first bitch outright, for by this method the purchaser may obtain the bitch with no down payment at all on the condition that he gives her erstwhile owner one or more of the puppies from her future litters. This sounds an ideal arrangement at first glance, but there are many snags in such an arrangement which should be considered carefully before the final steps are taken. The most obvious of these is that one can very seldom choose one's own animal; the owner usually has only one which he is willing to part with on these terms, and that probably either a 'left-over' which he has been unable to sell during puppyhood, or one which he had retained for himself but which had not fulfilled her early promise. In either case, the purchaser may well find himself landed with the type of animal he did not want at all in the first place. There are also a wide variety of terms in this type of arrangement, ranging from no cash payment at all plus, say, first and third choice of the bitch's first litter, to a substantial deposit followed by the pick of her first two or even three litters, in which latter case the purchaser has to wait a very long time indeed before he can really call his bitch his own, and pays in the long run several times her true value. In any event, it is as well to have all the terms clearly set forth in a signed agreement before entering into any such contract; such agreements can even be registered at the Kennel Club for a moderate fee, which, of course, provides the maximum safeguard against fraud for both parties. On the whole, however, the purchase of bitches on breeding terms is not a practice to be recommended, although I have myself been fortunate enough to obtain at least one first-class animal by this method, when my own funds were low and the owner was anxious to ensure that she would be able to obtain some of the bitch's future offspring.

CHOOSING THE STUD

Much has been written on this subject, with particular reference to the dangers of choosing 'the dog next door'; and in a comparatively rare breed like the Old English Sheepdog these dangers are magnified one hundred fold. For what could be easier—'Lassie's in season again! Oh, well—Mrs. So-and-so lives only twenty miles away, and she has a dog— ' This might be all very well for that fortunately rare animal, the breeder who has no other aim in life than to produce as many puppies as possible as quickly, easily, and cheaply as possible, and of no particular quality or merit, but it is easy to see that it is such breeders as these who bring the variety of their choice into general disrepute besides ultimately doing themselves a disservice by filling their kennels with poor stock which nobody wants. Most of us, fortunately, enter upon our career as breeders with a very definite urge either to produce a galaxy of champions or, at the least, to leave our mark in the form of some improvement in our own strain if nobody else's; and to this end it is imperative that we lay our plans with the utmost care and above all in plenty of time. It is no good waiting until your bitch is actually in season before you start to look round for a suitable mate for her; for months beforehand—in fact, as soon as you acquire your first bitch would not be too early—you would be well advised to visit the big Shows as often as you can, studying all the winning dogs, or, better still, the sires of winning dogs, and seeing which appeals most to your fancy. Having selected two or three, which you like the look of, you may now move one step nearer your ultimate goal by approaching their owners for details of pedigrees, so that you can judge how well these 'fit in' with your bitch's.

It is impossible here to delve too deeply into the realms of genetics; many books specializing in this subject, both generally and as applied to dogs in particular, are readily available. Furthermore, the more experienced breeder will know *a priori* that a certain strain has a tendency towards faulty mouths, another to light eyes, and a third is apt to throw a high proportion of brown or soft coats. For the beginner, however, it is broadly speaking sufficient that he should endeavour to find in his stud dog outstanding qualities to offset his bitch's faults. However good the bitch you buy, it is as well to remember that the perfect animal was never yet born—and very likely never will be!—so do not blind yourself to her poor bone, long muzzle, or indifferent hind action, but take care to choose for her mate a dog who excels in her weak points both within himself and in his progeny. His pedigree, too, should dovetail into hers. As your ambition will probably be one day to found a strain of your own, it would be a mistake to indulge in close in-breeding at the outset, as this would merely mean a slavish adherence to one already established by somebody else; but a certain degree of line breeding is generally advisable, as otherwise you may mate two animals of such widely divergent types that their offspring will probably be exceedingly indeterminate, and even at the worst a dreadful hodge-podge of most of the bad points of both parents! In any case, in-breeding should be practised only with superlatively sound stock, free from any really glaring faults, as all the qualities, both good and bad, will tend to be magnified in the resulting puppies. For the beginner, it might be as well to explain that in-breeding implies the mating of two very closely related animals, such as father to daughter, mother to son, or sister to brother, while line-breeding entails the mating of two animals with one or more less recent relative in common. The following pedigrees are examples of in-breeding and line-breeding which have been carried out in my own kennels.

It will be noted in comparing the two pedigrees (pp. 44 and 45) that Ch. Shepton Surf King and Ch. Shepton Perfect Picture, the G.G.G.-parents of Beanville Miss Bopeep, are descended from Boldwood Bombadier and Boldwood Bustle, and Nosey Parker of Pickhurst and Snow White of Pickhurst, who appear also as G.G.-parents of Amberford Rough and Ready. The dogs appearing in both sides of the pedigree of Amberford Cyrtel are shown in italics.

MATING

Assuming that you have already made up your mind which stud dog to use, it is a good plan to inform his owner of your intention and the approximate date when you are likely to be bringing your bitch along, for in most instances it is the bitch who has to visit the dog, although I cannot help feeling that the reverse procedure might have very definite advantages, particularly in the case of nervous or inexperienced females.

As soon as the bitch comes in season, you should contact the stud's owner once more, giving a more nearly accurate date this time. For the benefit of the beginner, it might be as well to explain here that the onset of the oestrus, or season, is first marked by the considerable swelling of the bitch's external genitalia, which may take place some days before she 'shows colour' in the form of a reddish discharge from the vagina. It is generally accepted that a bitch is ready for service twelve days after the commencement of this discharge, but in my experience no hard and fast ruling can be made, for I have known bitches to be mated successfully as late as the sixteenth day, while one Scottish Terrier bitch of mine was ready on the fourth! One thing *is* certain, and that is that she must have ceased to 'show colour' before being taken to the stud, but it is by far the best plan to see if she is ready to stand to a dog by introducing her (very carefully, of course!) to any dog near at hand and noting her reactions; if she hails him joyfully, and presents him with her rear end you may safely take it that she is ready—you may, in fact, rely on her to know the right day even if you don't!

A telegram of warning to the stud dog owner is now all that is necessary before you set off; if the journey is a long one, however, you would be well advised to stay overnight to give the bitch a good rest. I personally also think that two matings on subsequent days are advisable, for a bitch is usually ready to stand for at least three days, and it seems just possible that she may not be capable of conception on all of them. Many people, of course, *send* their bitches to the dog by rail; personally, I prefer to go along myself to see that all is well, but if you do decide to adopt this latter course, do remember that a bitch in season cannot travel safely unattended except in a hamper, and that this, in the case of a large breed like the Bobtail, must be of really huge dimensions to give her plenty of room and air. A little straw may be put on the floor to absorb excreta—but only a little, for large quantities very readily entangle themselves around a confined animal's limbs and may cause severe discomfort; a meaty bone will help her to while away the time; and, as it is obviously impossible to provide her with water on the journey, except through the ministrations of the railway staff, do be sure to give her a good drink before she embarks. When sending a bitch by rail, always be sure to notify the stud dog owner of her time of arrival to obviate a long wait on the station at the other end, and he will certainly notify you similarly when he returns her, usually after a few days during which she will have had ample time for plenty of rest and several matings.

If, on the other hand, you take your bitch personally to the stud, and have never undertaken such a mission before, you may well be rather startled by the proceedings if not forewarned, for the dog mates in a manner quite unlike that of any other mammal. It may, of course, take some time for the two animals to get to know each other at first, but, once the dog has mounted the bitch and successfully inserted his penis into the vagina, the male organ becomes enormously distended and, when the dog loosens his hold and is turned by his owner, the pair may remain 'tied' back to back for anything up to an hour, although about twenty minutes is the normal duration of this condition. During the 'tie' care must be taken to prevent the bitch from wandering

PEDIGREE OF AMBERFORD BUDICA (Example of Inbreeding, Nephew to Aunt)

Amberford Budica	Amberford Aethelbeald	Ch. Perrywood Sonny Boy	Prince Willow of Lyneal	Pastelblue King Willow	Cheddar of Pastelblue
					Boldwood Briar
				Faithful of the Hills	Pastelblue Cilsanws
					Jill of the Hills
			Perrywood Sunbonnet	Int. Ch. Shepton Sonny Boy of Marlay	Beau Brigand of Marlay
					Pastelblue Comedy Starlight
				Perrywood Lady Lynda of Yasabel	Julius of Bewkes
					Lady Prim
		Bridewell Ladies Model	Int. Ch. Shepton Sonny Boy of Marlay	Beau Brigand of Marlay	Shepton Franconia
					Romance
				Pastelblue Comedy Starlight	The Squyer of Fullson
					Powder Puff of Pastorale
			Ch. Shepton Lovely Memory	Ch. Shepton Surf King	Boldwood Bombadier
					Boldwood Bustle
				Ch. Shepton Perfect Picture	Nosey Parker of Pickhurst
					Snow White of Pickhurst
	Bridewell Lovely Maiden	Int. Ch. Shepton Sonny Boy of Marlay	Beau Brigand of Marlay	Shepton Franconia	Shepton Pride of the Hills
					Shepton Suzette
				Romance	Shepton Grey Dawn
					Shepton Morning Glory
			Pastelblue Comedy Starlight	The Squyer of Fullson	Ch. Tom Noddy of Pastorale
					Ch. Pastoral Mistress of Fullson
				Powder Puff of Pastorale	Shaggy Shoes of Pastorale
					Mistress Mulisande of Pastorale
		Ch. Shepton Lovely Memory	Ch. Shepton Surf King	Boldwood Bombadier	Bonny Blue Boy
					Blue Belle of Anstey
				Boldwood Bustle	The Sword of Pastorale
					Boldwood Ballad
			Ch. Shepton Perfect Picture	Nosey Parker of Pickhurst	Dane of Pickhurst
					Hamara
				Snow White of Pickhurst	Toby of Pickhurst
					Lady Lightening of Pickhurst

PEDIGREE OF AMBERFORD CYRTEL (Example of Line Breeding)

Amberford Cyrtel	Amberford Rough and Ready	Watchers Ring Leader	Peter Joseph of Pickhurst	*Nosey Parker of Pickhurst*
				Dane of Pickhurst
				Hamara
				Snow White of Pickhurst
				Toby of Pickhurst
				Lady Lightening of Pickhurst
			Watchers Grey Dawn	Eskgrove Glyn
				Eskgrove Chance
				Newcote October Blossom
				Eskgrove Becky
				Ch. Tom Noddy of Pastorale
				Ch. Thyrza
		Patricia of Littleparc	King Spiv	Boldwood Bulwark
				The Sword of Pastorale
				Boldwood Blossom
				Lady Blue
				Pastelblue Mike
				Blue Biddy of Lynhaven
			Boldwood Bombette	*Boldwood Bombadier*
				Bonny Blue Boy
				Blue Belle of Anstey
				Boldwood Bustle
				The Sword of Pastorale
				Boldwood Ballad
	Beanville Miss Bopeep	Ch. Roderick of Squarefour	Gordale Grey Guardsman	Watchers Grey Monarch
				Watchers Warrant
				Watchers Grey Dawn
				Jill of the Hills
				Master Donald of Halliwick
				Contrary Mary
			Priscilla of Squarefour	Shepton Brave Boy
				Boldwood Bombadier
				Pride of Yeldhams
				Prudence of Squarefour
				Saffwalden Eskgrove Bushey
				Pastelblue Topnotcher
		Amberford Aclea	Ch. Perrywood Sonny Boy	Prince Willow of Lyneal
				Pastelblue King Willow
				Faithful of the Hills
				Perrywood Sunbonnet
				Int. Ch. Shepton Sonny Boy of Marlay
				Perrywood Lady Lynda of Yasabel
			Bridewell Ladies Model	Int. Ch. Shepton Sonny Boy of Marlay
				Beau Brigand of Marlay
				Pastelblue Comedy Starlight
				Ch. Shepton Lovely Memory
				Ch. Shepton Surf King
				Ch. Shepton Perfect Picture.

away, thus dragging the dog after her, or the dog from lying down, for both seem to become throughly bored with this part of the proceedings, and serious injury to the dog might well result from any sudden movement on the part of either. Should you, later on, keep a stud dog yourself, you may find it necessary to assist him by guiding him manually into the vagina, but this is best learned from experience, and cannot easily be described.

In brief, the main points to look out for with a view to a successful mating are as follows:

(*a*) Look out for the beginning of the oestrus—this is not always readily apparent in a long-coated breed such as the Old English Sheepdog.

(*b*) Try to make the mating as natural as possible—give the animals time to become acquainted, and I personally do not advocate forced matings where the bitch obviously disapproves of your choice of stud; generally speaking, such matings do not appear to be eminently successful, but in any case one should remember that dogs are individuals and not merely puppy-producing automatons, and surely their own wishes should be consulted to some extent in such matters.

(*c*) Take no notice of the advisers who advocate a particular stud because he sired umpteen puppies in his last three litters—unless the dog is virtually sterile, it is the bitch who determines the size of the litter, and the most fertile dog on earth cannot make her conceive more puppies than the number of ripe ova she has produced.

CARE OF THE IN-WHELP BITCH

Because bitches carry their puppies very high up in the body, it is sometimes very difficult to determine definitely whether or not they are actually in whelp right up to the birth itself; we remarked one day that a certain bitch of ours, who had been mated unknown to us, was rather thin—and the following day found that she had produced five puppies! So, once your bitch has been mated, it is as well to consider her in whelp, whatever her appearance, until she has proved to be otherwise.

For the first five or six weeks after mating (the gestation period of the dog is approximately sixty-three days) this entails no special care, but for the last three or four weeks of pregnancy an enriched diet is to be advocated to prevent the unborn litter from making too great demands upon the resources of the mother. As the digestive organs now tend to become compressed as the distended uterus occupies more room, several small meals each day are preferable to one big one; and the addition of such items as milk, eggs, and codliver oil all help towards the production of fine, healthy puppies from a fine, healthy dam. As a great deal of calcium is required in the bone formation of the youngsters, this should be added in some more concentrated form as a supplement to that already present in the diet, and personally I have found nothing better than lime-water. One or two tablespoonsful added to a tasty meal (the undisguised flavour is none too palatable!) will work wonders, provided that codliver oil is given also, as the one cannot be fully utilized in the dog's body chemistry without the other.

In the matter of exercise, the bitch may very well be left to use her own discretion, although she should not be encouraged to leap about too much in the later stages, nor to insert herself into tight corners. The day before one of my bitches, who slept in our bedroom, whelped, we were awakened during the night by our large double bed behaving something like a ship on a stormy night, and discovered that the poor creature had crawled under it to sleep and now, firmly wedged, was literally bouncing us—and it—up and down in her efforts to extricate herself. Possibly as a result of this escapade, her litter was born within the next twenty-four hours just five days prematurely.

CHAPTER 5

WHELPING AND PUPPY REARING

He could run among the flower-heads without injuring a single plant, and at Compton Abdale one day took a four-foot stream with a wall of the same height on the farther bank at a single desultory bound. One would never have suspected what a soundless, elegant runner he was, with an easy, tireless, rhythmic canter that could carry him for miles. . . .

He never provoked any of his fellows, but no living dog could take advantage of him. With a child (and all children adored him) he would play by the hour, and for all his force and stature never exhibit a moment's roughness, whereas when I was engaged with him, it was like withstanding the onset of a young elephant.

H. J. MASSINGHAM

(Description of a Cotswold Sheepdog from *Wold without End.*)

About ten days before the estimated date of the birth of the puppies, preparations for their reception should begin in earnest. Although the official gestation period of the dog is sixty-three days, individuals may deviate very considerably from this, the longest deviation which I know of personally being in the case of a bitch who whelped ten lovely big puppies, showing no signs of prematurity, exactly one week early. It is, therefore, better to be safe than sorry, and start your final arrangements in good time. The bitch should first be clipped (see page 29), either entirely or at the very least over the area surrounding her genitalia and mammary glands; and these parts should be thoroughly cleansed with a mild solution of some harmless antiseptic such as Dettol to prevent possible uterine infection after the birth or the absorption of worm ova by the suckling young.

The next step is to decide where the happy event is to take place, and should this be somewhere to which the bitch is not accustomed, to install her in her new quarters so that she will not be upset and uneasy in strange surroundings during the actual confinement. Personally I much prefer to let my bitches whelp in the house, where an even temperature can most easily be maintained, and the human attendants can carry out their duties with the maximum ease and comfort. With reasonable care this procedure need not entail any serious degree of mess, for the dam will keep her young meticulously clean for the first two or three weeks, and, providing that she is well house-trained, is unlikely to have any 'accidents' herself. Certainly the comforts of a warm fire and cosy armchair make a possible all-night vigil infinitely more pleasant than it would be if one was squatting on the floor of an ill-lit kennel! Having selected the room, then, one should now turn one's attention to making up a suitable bed; for such a large breed as the Bobtail I have found that a wooden whelping box as recommended for many smaller breeds tends to be somewhat unwieldy, and so generally simplify matters by merely allotting one draught-free corner to the expectant mother. Here I spread a large ground sheet covered with a liberal supply of old newspapers and top the whole off with a layer of clean sacking or an old blanket—not *too* old, though, for newly born puppies are apt to squirm through any holes in their search for food and so may easily be suffocated or overlaid by their mother. As the onset of parturition often arouses a spasm of destructiveness in even the most docile bitch, who may tear up anything within reach in her instinct to 'make a bed' for the occasion, it is advisable to remove all your more treasured possessions, particularly cushions and the like, well out of harm's way, when you may now sit back and await the incipient event with equanimity.

In order to ensure that you are available at the time of the actual birth, it is a wise precaution to take the bitch's temperature every day during the week prior to the expected date of whelping; the normal temperature of the dog varies between

100·5 and 101·5 degrees F., but during this period it is usual for the bitch's to fall to 99 degrees, or even less, a further drop of one or two degrees being noted when whelping is imminent. Should her temperature *rise* before whelping, your veterinary surgeon should be consulted, as this may well indicate that all is not as it should be. When, in conjunction with a low temperature, the bitch starts to pant, shiver, scratch up her bedding, refuse food, and generally become thoroughly restless and ill at ease, you may confidently expect labour to start at any moment, and a close watch should be kept from now on to see that all goes well.

In a normal whelping the actual labour, with the bitch straining to expel each puppy, does not take very long, although there may well be lengthy intervals between each birth, but should she continue to strain for an hour or so with no puppy being born, veterinary advice should be sought immediately. Most manuals on dog breeding advocate as little interference as possible, stating that the bitch prefers to be left alone, and hates to see her puppies handled; personally I have found that my bitches, possibly because they are all 'friends of the family' and not merely kennel breeding machines, welcome a certain amount of companionship at this time, and appear actively to enjoy having their offspring admired. Nor do I advocate removing each puppy to a warmed box as it is born; in spite of their size and apparent clumsiness most Bobtails are adept at avoiding stepping on their young ones, and only while a second puppy is actually being born do I ever attempt to move the first out of harm's way. I am also of the opinion that many breeders tend to coddle their stock unnecessarily; with her heavy coat, the bitch is well equipped to withstand quite low temperatures both for herself and the puppies she is nursing, and overheating seems to me to have quite as many dangers as its opposite. Certainly I would provide heat for a bitch whelping in a kennel during the winter, but ordinary comfortable room temperature is quite sufficient and can generally be induced by the suspension of an infra-red lamp some four or five feet above the 'nest' in otherwise unheated quarters.

As the whelping of a large litter—anything up to ten or twelve is quite common in this breed—is a hard and exhausting task, it is a good idea to offer the bitch drinks of warm milk between puppies; I have heard it said that *warm* milk tends to dull the labour pains and so delay subsequent births, but have personally never found this to be the case, and can definitely state from personal experience in childbirth that warm liquids are more palatable than cold! When not busy cleaning and cuddling her puppies, she may, especially if she is a household pet, appreciate a little petting and comforting herself at this time; it is also often said that the suckling of the first puppies tends to hasten the birth of those who follow after, but I find it best to respect the bitch's own wishes in this matter, as some seem definitely to resent feeding any of their young ones until all are present to join in the feast.

Normally the bitch can be relied upon to deal with each puppy as it is born, but occasionally a maiden bitch will apparently be at a loss to know what to do with this startling new arrival; one bitch of mine was quite nonplussed by her first born, but watched with interest while I carefully drew the foetal membrane away from its head and later cut the cord—she was a quick learner and coped perfectly with all the subsequent puppies! Should it fall to your lot to perform these duties, you will find it surprisingly easy to rupture the membrane, or bag, in which every puppy is born, when it usually immediately draws its first breath with a strange whimpering wail; should it show no signs of breathing, however, this can usually be induced by gently opening the mouth with one's little finger and, in extreme cases, drawing the tongue well forward and blowing into the empty lungs. Lightly tossing the puppy from hand to hand will also often encourage regular respiration in a whelp which is breathing only spasmodically. Having ensured that the puppy is alive and breathing normally, you should next cut the cord which will still be attaching it to the placenta or afterbirth Sterilized cotton should first be tied tightly round the cord on the side nearest to the puppy, however, and on both sides of the cut if the placenta has not yet been expelled from the mother's body. Only about one inch of the cord should be left attached to the puppy's umbilicus. In the case of the dog, incidentally, there is one placenta for each foetus, and it is most important to see that all these come away from the dam, as the retention of one, or even part of one, may result in metritis. (see page 78) with disastrous results. If you are in the least doubtful about whether or not all the placentas have come away, an injection of pituitrin after the birth of all the puppies will obviate any risk. As the bitch normally devours each placenta after biting through the umbilical cord—a practice not to be interfered with as it is thought that the placenta has a medicinal effect beneficial to the dam—it is not so easy to keep count as one might at first suppose, so when in doubt—

Soon after the last puppy is born, the bitch usually likes to go outside to relieve herself, and while she is thus occupied, the now sodden bedding may well be renewed so that she returns to find her family cosily ensconced on a clean, dry blanket. On the whole, Sheepdogs do not tend to be clumsy with their young, and seldom lie or step on them, so a day and night watch is seldom necessary, as is the case with some breeds. Providing that the dam's milk supply is adequate, you may now safely leave the puppies entirely in her care for several weeks to come, only ensuring that she herself has a rich and nutritious diet to meet the demands they make upon her. It is generally advocated that a bitch be kept on 'slops' for a few days after whelping, but I have found that her return to a normal meat diet may safely be left to her own discretion—speaking again from personal experience, the newly-delivered mother is generally ravenously hungry, and I should have greatly resented being offered rice pudding when I was ready for a beef steak, so I give my bitches meat as soon as they are prepared to take it, and have discovered that when they are not there is usually something wrong. Certainly the best milk producing foods for the nursing bitch appear to be raw meat and milk, which she should be given separately and in large quantities, several times each day. Her diet may also be enriched with eggs or fish, as during her pregnancy, and, of course, lime water and codliver oil are now even more essential than before.

BOTTLE FEEDING

Sometimes, due to the death or illness of the bitch, or merely to poor or even total lack of lactation, it becomes necessary either to bottle feed the puppies or lose the entire litter. Although this is an onerous task, it is also a rewarding one, and may be very successful if tackled sensibly. Unfortunately, many people are far from sensible, and, by following the light of their own ignorance, bring their efforts to complete failure and, by advertising the fact, throw the whole practice of bottle-rearing into disrepute.

The chief cause for most of the dismal failures in this direction lies in the lack of knowledge of the constitution of bitches' milk. For some reason, presumably because a cow is a large animal, many people (and not a few of them ought to know better) attempt to rear puppies on diluted cows' milk alone. Now, it so happens that bitches' milk is one of the richest of all mammals', while the cow's is one of the weakest, so it is quite obvious that a puppy's digestive system is not adapted to derive sufficient nourishment even from pure cows' milk, and still less when it has been watered down. The following analysis of various kinds of milk will show what I mean.

Animal	*Sugar*	*Casein, etc.*	*Fat*	*Salts*	*Water*
Dog	3·1	8·0	12·0	1·2	75·5
Goat	4·75	4·0	6·25	1·0	84·0
Cat	5·2	7·9	3·65	0·9	82·35
Cow	4·85	3·75	3·7	0·6	87·1
Sheep	4·95	4·7	5·2	0·7	84·45

For successful bottle feeding, then, cows' milk must be *enriched*, and I have found the following recipe enimently efficient both in keeping the whelps alive, and in laying the foundations of really good stock in later years. First of all you require one large tin of some brand of full cream baby food, such as Ostermilk, and one smaller tin of Slippery Elm Food, by volume rather more than twice as much of the former as the latter. These two powders are now thoroughly blended, and one teaspoonful of the mixture, together with one teaspoonful of honey mixed smoothly with the cream off one pint bottle of cows' milk. The resulting glutinous mess is best warmed to blood heat by the container in which it had been made up being stood in a pan of boiling water, which latter commodity will later prove invaluable in cleansing both the puppies and yourself! Each newly born puppy will take from two to three teaspoonsful of this mixture at each feed, (by the time weaning commences, this may well have increased to as many tablespoons) and, having experimented with practically every type of feeder on the market, I have come to the conclusion that the best way of administering the food is by means of an ordinary teaspoon. The puppy is held on one's lap with the left hand, his head being directed *away* from one, and the left index finger, preferably smeared with the mixture, is inserted into his mouth. The puppy usually at once begins to suck this finger vigorously, and, as he does so, the food is trickled into his mouth slowly from the spoon held in the right hand. This method of feeding has the advantage of being considerably less messy than most, and also, I feel, must appear more natural to the infant, who is thus apparently obtaining his nourishment by sucking at something composed of warm flesh. Should you, incidentally, find yourself landed with an orphan litter and no puppy-rearing food, the whelps may be kept alive on warm glucose and water until the food is obtained.

The major drawback to bottle feeding is, of course, that your charges will require nutriment at regular intervals both day and night; at first this interval should not exceed every three hours, but may be reduced to every four hours after about ten days, while the 'middle-of-the-night' feed may be dropped altogether when the puppies are a fortnight old. If the cause of the bottle rearing is not the actual death of the dam, she may still be available to keep the litter warm, as well as washing their faces and 'changing their nappies'. If this is not the case, however, it is most important to remember to wipe the whelps clean with a piece of cotton wool wrung out in hot water after each feed, and also to massage their abdomens and excretory organs to induce the passage of faeces and urine. Between feeds, they should be kept in a warm basket, preferably under an infra red lamp—but *not* one of that variety which gives off a dazzling white glare, as this is both bad for their eyes, when these open, and also tends to overheat them.

WEANING

The puppies' eyes normally open when they are about ten days old; they begin to crawl about soon after the fortnight; and they should be removed to a kennel (slightly heated if in winter) at the age of three to four weeks if your carpets are not to suffer, as about this time the bitch ceases to 'change nappies' and the first of a myriad pools and messes begin to appear. At four weeks, too, weaning may commence—or even earlier if the litter is so big that the dam's strength is in danger of being undermined, although in my experience Bobtails appear to be quite capable of rearing really large litters without supplementary feeding for the puppies during the early stages. Most manuals on dog breeding devote a great deal of space to the subject of weaning, and, in my opinion, tend to magnify it into a far more difficult problem than is in fact the case. I am myself a great believer that most dogs have a great deal more sense in matters canine than have their owners, and consequently I try to be guided so far as is possible by the animals' own wishes on any subject pertaining to them. In the matter of weaning, then, I decide to start operations when the puppies themselves announce their readiness for this step by elbowing their mother away from her own dish and making merry with its contents! Mother's meat is, of course, usually cut into portions too large to be dealt with satisfactorily by her offspring's tiny mouths and teeth, so I do *not* encourage them all to eat *en famille*; there is also the danger of a really good dam starving herself in order to allow her family to indulge in sheer greed, which is good for neither party, so as soon as the puppies show a desire for solid food I start feeding them separately, but on a diet very much the same as that which their mother has been receiving for the previous seven o eight weeks. To begin with the whelps are given five meals each day, and a balanced diet is ensured by the inclusion of raw meat, cereals, eggs, gravy, codliver oil, and lime water. The following is a satisfactory menu for newly weaned puppies:

Breakfast: Thick porridge beaten up with raw eggs and milk.
Lunch: Chopped raw meat.
Tea: Brown bread and milk.

Dinner: Brown bread soaked in gravy, raw meat, codliver oil, and lime water.
Supper: Milk, with or without eggs.

Personally I have not found it necessary to scrape, pound, or mince raw meat for even the youngest puppies; provided it is cut into small enough pieces it will be devoured eagerly and with no ill effects. Nor have I found it necessary to introduce new foods very gradually; while the puppies are still feeding very regularly from their dam, I generally start them off with only about three meals each day, say breakfast, dinner, and supper, and add more meals as they seem necessary, but I have yet to have a puppy fall ill through too sudden a change in diet. When the youngsters are ready for solids, they will tell you so by starting to steal their mother's, and at that stage it seems to be a case of a little of what they fancy doing them good, so do not be scared by old wives' tales or look upon weaning with grave apprehension as some sort of ghastly obstacle race with death! When the puppies are ten weeks old, one meal may be dropped, and another at four months, but it is best to continue with two or three meals each day until they are at least one year old, for the Bobtail is a big dog, and has to develop into such from a tiny creature weighing only about one pound at birth, so that he does not reach full maturity as early as do dogs of smaller breeds and consequently requires 'building up' for a longer period.

DOCKING

Although a few Old English Sheepdogs are born with no tails, the vast majority have to have these appendages removed by docking at an early age. This operation is not so terrible as it may sound, provided that you are lucky enough, as I am, to have a really good veterinary surgeon to do the job—I have known vets who simply slash off the tail without preamble, and then leave the unfortunate puppy to bleed to death or not as its luck may be! I generally have my puppies docked when they are three or four days old, and each is given a local anaesthetic at the root of the tail before this is carefully removed as close to the body as possible. The raw stump is then cauterized to remove any risk of

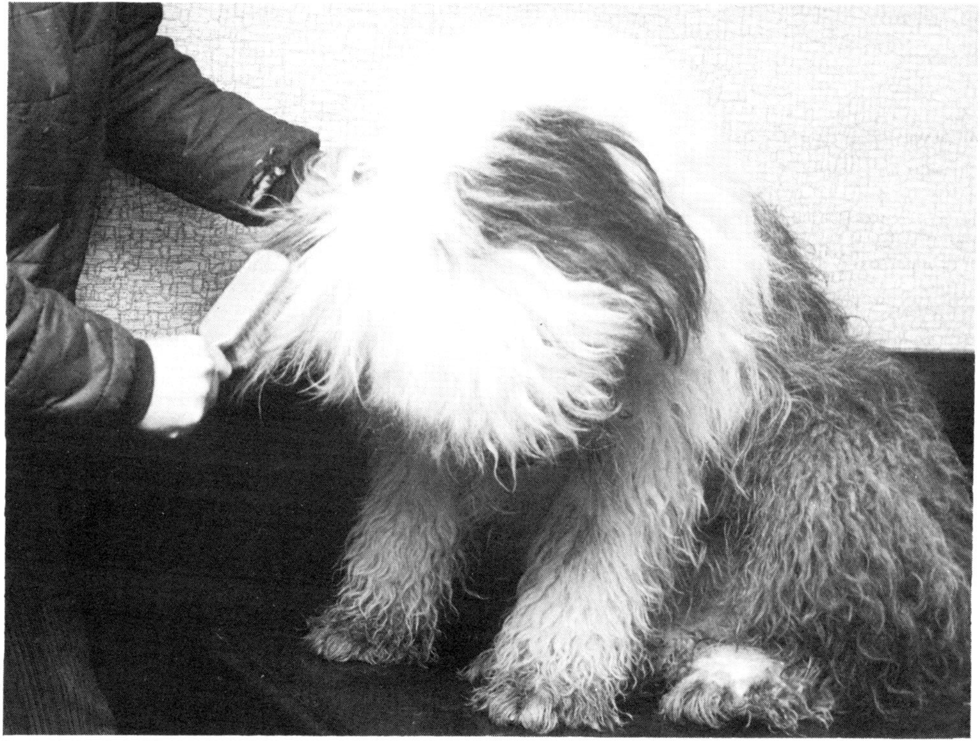

Old English Sheepdog being groomed with brush

All from same Cinderwood litter
owners Mrs. Siddall, Dr. A. Hodgson, Mr. Selva

haemorrhage, the dew claws are quickly removed at the same time, and the whole litter is very soon once more happily suckling from their dam as if nothing had happened. Needless to say, the operation must always be carried out well away from the bitch's quarters; I usually send mine out for a walk during the veterinary surgeon's visit so that there is no chance of her seeing or hearing anything of the proceedings.

WORMING

Virtually all puppies seem to have worms, though fortunately these are usually only of the round variety. It is, therefore, a good plan to worm the whole litter when they are about six weeks old, before they are sold to new homes where their purchasers may not be aware of this danger. Personally I always get my veterinary surgeon to leave me a suitable quantity of vermifuge when he comes to dock the puppies' tails, rather than relying on a random choice of one of the myriad proprietary brands which are always on the market.

SELLING YOUR PUPPIES

As Bobtails are not among the fashionably popular breeds, such as Poodles, or even the regular 'good sellers' such as Scottish Terriers, you are unlikely to find homes for the whole litter with your first advertisement. It is, therefore, a good plan to start advertising them at an early age, say six weeks, and continue to do so regularly until the last one goes, perhaps at twice that age. If your bitch and the puppies' sire are well known in the Show ring, you will probably do best by putting your advertisements in the canine periodicals, but otherwise you are probably more likely to get results through the medium of one of your local newspapers, particularly if you live in an area where the Old English Sheepdog is a rarity and the demand thus not yet satiated. If your aim is to breed champions, you will, of course, prefer your puppies to go to homes where they will be shown; certainly you will have a few at least who can be sold for nothing but pets; some may be sought by farmers who want them primarily in their original capacity as sheep or cattle dogs. But, into whichever category your stock or their prospective purchasers may fall, do, I beg of you, do everything in your power to see that the youngsters go only to really *good* homes, for the Bobtail is a dog who needs a great deal of love and attention, and, as I have explained in another chapter, an ungroomed, unloved, uncared for Sheepdog is a sight to rouse pity in even the hardest hearted non-dog-lover.

CHAPTER 6

SHOWING

With eye upraised, his master's looks to scan,
The joy, the solace, and the aid of man,
The rich man's guardian, and the poor man's friend,
The only creature faithful to the end.

GEORGE CRABBE

Many people, of course, buy a puppy merely as a pet; but it is surprising how many of these are tempted by admirers of their dog to enter him at some small local Show and, having perhaps gained a couple of cards there, find that the thrill of showing is in their blood, and so go on from strength to strength. So, if you are one of those for whom their Old English Sheepdog is no more than a first rate friend and companion, do not be too sure that this chapter can never apply to you!

Too many chapters on showing dogs in books similar to this start and end with a detailed list of what one should do to prepare one's exhibit, thus leaving the unfortunate novice completely in the dark as to actual show procedure; let us, therefore, put first things first, and discover to begin with just how one finds out when and where a show is taking place, and how one enters for it. Perhaps the best initial move for the would-be showman is to write to the Kennel Club for a copy of their Rules and Regulations; this supplies all possible information about every aspect of the cult of the pedigree dog from the registration of puppies to the duties of stewards, as well as giving a wealth of information about all the various different kinds of Show. It is not possible, except at Exemption Shows, to exhibit a dog which has not first been registered at the Kennel Club, and the registration subsequently transferred to the present owner, so do make sure that you receive your puppy's registration certificate and a signed transfer form along with the animal, unless, of course, his breeder failed to register him when you can do so yourself on a form supplied by the Kennel Club. As the number of Challenge Certificates available to a breed is decided by the number of registrations, I should like here to put in a special plea to breeders to register their stock; it is to the advantage of all concerned that whole litters be registered soon after birth.

Having a promising young puppy of six months or so, then, duly registered and transferred to your name, you are now eager to start him on his career—but where, when, and how? The best move at this stage is to become a subscriber to one of the weekly canine papers, either *Our Dogs* or *Dog World,* where all the forthcoming shows are regularly advertised, and you will probably be pleasantly surprised to find how many are available within quite a short distance of your home. To start with, it is always best to enter your dog at a small Sanction Show, where he and you will be able to learn the art of showing together for only a modest entry fee, without having to travel long distances, and probably being away from home for only half an afternoon instead of a whole day as would be the case with a Championship or Open Show. While the Sanction Show is an excellent training ground both for the dog and the exhibitor, however, it is only fair to point out that the Old English Sheepdogs very seldom have separate classification at such events, and consequently have to be entered in Variety Classes, where you may well find yourself competing against Chihuahuas, Whippets, and Bedlington Terriers, so it is as well not to be too much cast down by failure or elated by success unless the judge happens to be one of the first flight, as most of the lesser lights seem, in my experience, to have a tendency to allot places only to representatives of those breeds which they know best and can therefore *really* judge and assess for merit. Also, as the Bobtail tends to mature very slowly he is at a disadvantage in mixed Puppy Classes where some at least of his competitors may well have already achieved the coat and conformation of an adult in their particular breed. Nevertheless, although his success or lack of it at Sanction Shows may give no very reliable indication of his future chances in Breed Classes, any puppy destined for a Show career will benefit immeasurably from occasional entries at Sanction Shows, so that his first engagement will not find him nervous, ring-shy, or completely unaware of what is expected of him.

When you have scanned through all the advertisements and decided at which Show you mean to make your debut, the next move is to write to the secretary, whose name and address will always be supplied in the advertisement, for a schedule, which will doubtless at first seem to offer you a bewildering selection of possible classes in which to enter your prodigy. At this stage always try to apply the golden rule of showing your dog only in competition with his peers, either according to age or previous Show success; thus an untried youngster of seven or eight months might best be entered in Special Puppy (six to nine months), Puppy (six to twelve months), or Maiden (never having won a first prize). Such classes as A.V. (Any Variety) Non-sporting, A.V. Owned and Handled by a Lady, or A.V. Not Bred by Exhibitor are best left alone until you have learnt to know the ropes and properly assess the quality of your exhibit, as they are also open to the galaxy of big winners whose owners will almost certainly be attracted to enter in them. Before you send in your entry form do be careful to check it for errors—make doubly sure that you have put down the right numbers of the classes you have chosen and that your dog's sire, dam, date of birth, and the breeder are given correctly; otherwise you may find yourself entered in a class for which you are ineligible (and you can be penalized for this), or fall foul of the breeder if the dog does well and he or she find themselves incorrectly named in the catalogue! I have, incidentally, known this to happen even at Championship Shows, where the loss in the first instance is considerable, while in the second the breeder in question was most annoyed.

Having sent off your entry with the *right* fees and before the closing date, all you have to do before the great day is to remember the date and place of the event. Assuming that you *have* remembered both correctly, you should take care to arrive in good time, so that a mad rush at the last minute will not upset your dog, and you will be able to prepare him for the ring at your leisure when you have discovered which part of the Hall or grounds has been set aside for this purpose. Do, please, adhere to the requests of the Show Committee on this point, for many good Halls are now being refused for Dog Shows owing to some people's lack of consideration in leaving a trail of chalk and dog hair in every corner. On arrival at the Show venue, your first task will be to have your dog vetted; this is essential to avoid so far as possible any risk of infection from other dogs, and should never be dodged; unfortunately, at many small Shows, and even some Championship events, such dodging is all too easy, but when you realize that one day some other dodger might well bring infection to *your* exhibit you will, I am sure, agree that it is only 'playing the game' to make sure that your own is examined and passed as fit by the veterinary surgeon always in attendance. Your only other duties at any Show are to keep your ears and eyes open for the commencement of your classes and to see that your exhibit is brought into the ring promptly; once in the ring, keep your attention on your dog and the judge; do as the judge or steward tells you, and, once you have passed under scrutiny, keep your wits about you so that, if you are placed, you do not find yourself fiddling about titivating up your exhibit instead of moving promptly into the place allotted to you! In fact, all too many Shows, and especially Sanction Shows, fail to start on time, and I cannot help feeling that if everybody took the above advice this need not be the case. However, provided that you yourself are on time, although you may well be irritated by the delay caused by the tardiness of others, at least you will not have been guilty of such gross discourtesy both to the other exhibitors and the judge.

So much for the part played by the exhibitor in this Show business—but what of the exhibit? First and foremost it is imperative to realize that, if you hope to get to the top, it is no good starting to prepare your dog for showing the day before the event, or even the day on which you send off your entries. To be in first rate show condition, a Bobtail must receive attention every day of the year; his coat must be impeccable, his health perfect, his training, housing, and feeding always of the best. No amount of last-minute grooming will restore an undercoat torn out by months of injudicious combing, no sudden spate of beef steaks put substance into a body which has been undernourished for years. The time to start building the future Champion is before he is born, when his mother's diet may well make all the difference to his bone and constitution, as it will continue to do so while she is suckling him. After weaning, a superlatively good diet, with plenty of meat and milk, is essential during the first twelve to eighteen months of his life, and even after that poor feeding or lack of free exercise will very quickly cause a lowering of general condition and so loss of bloom vitality. The coat of the newly born puppy is short, smooth, and black; as soon as this starts to grow to any appreciable length—say during the third or fourth month—daily brushing may well aid its development as well as hastening the casting of the puppy coat and substitution of the blue or grey harsh coat of the adult. This change of coat *may* take place before the youngster is six months old, but is more frequently delayed much longer and might even not be completed at eighteen months, so do not despair if you have to enter a black Old English Sheepdog at his first Show—judges make allowance for such colouration at least as long as the animal is eligible for Puppy Classes, and will be unlikely to penalize him for it. When selecting a very young puppy with an eye to future showing, it is, I have found, all too easy to be misled by his markings, which are, of course, very noticeable, to the detriment of other and more important points. Remember that the Standard states that the Bobtail shall be 'any shade of grey, grizzle, blue, or blue merle, with or without white markings, or in reverse', and makes no stipulation at all concerning the *position* of such markings, so that talk of 'mismarked' Sheepdogs is absolutely ridiculous. At the moment, all-white heads are very much in vogue, and these do indeed look very attractive and showy, other things being equal, but the puppy with the biggest head, best bone, shortest back, etc., may well be one with very little white on it at all, and should by no means be turned down on this account. Entirely white Sheepdogs also have been bred and are not frowned upon while allowance is also made in the Standard for wholly grey specimens, although I have never heard of one.

Assuming that your dog has been 'Champion-reared' from birth, with plenty of good food, grooming, and exercise, the preparations specifically directed towards his success at any given Show should not be very exacting. Almost certainly his white parts at least will require washing, and I usually do this on the morning of the day before the Show. Although I have heard of owners who bath each foot and finally the head separately in a bowl or pail, I have personally found this procedure most messy and unsatisfactory, and generally wash mine in a shallow bath, taking care that as little of the main body coat as possible gets wet. Apart from this variation, the normal bathing method as given in Chapter Three is followed, a blue-bag being dissolved in the final rinsing water to add just that little extra gleam to the already near-perfect whiteness. By bathing the dog in the morning, I ensure that he is dry by the evening, when I undertake his grooming, I find that this can be carried out with fewer interruptions when the normal day's work is over, the children in bed —they *love* 'helping'!—and my husband available to hold the animal if necessary or collect Show leads and make sandwiches to my specification as I work. The only major difference between grooming for Show and ordinary grooming is that the former needs to be just that little bit more thorough; not even the tiniest clot must be allowed to remain anywhere—even those ticklish spots round the toes or the genitalia cannot be skimped this time, and, to judge by their panting, the operation appears to be nearly as wearying for the dog as his owner! When the brushing is completed to your satisfaction, so that every hair seems to stand out from a froth of fluffly undercoat, I find it a good idea to give a liberal application of powdered chalk, of which there are several reputable brands on the market, over the entire body; this seems to bring out the blue tones in the body coat while, of course, enhancing the white parts still further, and, if the whiskers have become stained with food, as is often the case, I smother them in a paste made from ordinary whitening. This dissolves away when the dog takes his next drink, leaving the hair pure and unsullied. The final stages of grooming are, of course, undertaken at the Show itself. Here, if it be an Open or Championship event, tables are usually provided so that these can be carried out with the maximum convenience, and it is as well to join the queue for their use as soon as you have found your bench and deposited your goods there. (At benched Shows a permanent 'spot' is allocated to each dog in the form of a raised trestle table divided into compartments of size suitable for the breed in question, and here the dog should remain, on view to all visitors whenever he is not in the ring, or being groomed or exercised.) During the final grooming, after a quick once over to ensure that no clots escaped your notice the previous evening, your main task is to brush the coat up to its greatest glory, possibly once more chalking the white parts; to achieve the correct shape, the hair on the shoulders should be brushed *down,* while that on the hind legs, rump, and loins is brushed *up and out*; the hair on the ears may be brushed up and then, lightly, down again to exaggerate the width of the skull, some of that on the neck being brushed forwards with similar effect. To whiten the feet a bag filled with french chalk is very useful, as the entire lower leg can be inserted into it and the powder worked into the coat with the fingers, while I find a chalk block excellent to rub into the whiskers or elbows where discoloured hair is most commonly found.

As is the case with most subjects which require practical application, a little experience is far more valuable than endless book-learning, and watching others grooming their dogs will teach the novice far more about the necessary technique than could any words of mine. Very often, fortunately, the breeder of his puppy will also be a Show-goer, and only too ready to assist his efforts at his first big Show, but should this not be so, he would be well advised to request the co-operation of his bench neighbour, when he is most likely to receive all the help he requires.

When you go into the ring, always take a brush with you so that the fall may be brushed down again after the judge has examined your dog's eyes, or the hair on his rump quickly brought up into position should it become flattened by handling. Although the Bobtail may need a great deal of attention to keep him and his massive coat in Show condition, one point on which he scores, in my opinion, over other breeds is that he requires very little 'handling' in the ring; when one sees some Terrier or Gundog handlers crouching awkwardly to hold their exhibit's tails, legs, or other outlying parts in the correct position, one is grateful that all one has to do to show off one's own is to raise him fore and aft and let him drop back into what should be his natural stance, with front legs dead straight and parallel and hind legs placed squarely well apart. Keep his head well up (this can usually be achieved merely by talking to him) and, provided that he has been taught to stand reasonably still in the ring, you have nothing more to worry about. When moving the dog, try to teach him to go well on a slack lead and with no bounding or leaping about, although many Sheepdogs are so full of vitality that this may not be easy, and such behaviour is in any case not severely penalized. Above all, do not be *too* disappointed if you fail to bring home a red card; although most dog folk are pleasant people, there are always a few bad losers who storm out of the ring without congratulating the winner of the Challenge Certificate, and it is such as they who bring the dog game to ill repute—for it *is* only a game, remember, and *too* serious a view of it is liable to breed more bad blood than good dogs.

CHAPTER 7

AILMENTS

The misery of keeping a dog is his dying so soon; but to be sure if he loved for fifty years, and then died, what would become of me?

SIR WALTER SCOTT

The vast list of ailments given in many dog books might well lead the prospective owner of one of these animals into the erroneous belief that his new pet was more likely to be a liability than an asset, always having something wrong with him and constantly in need of veterinary attention. In fact, of course, the dog is a remarkably hardy animal, and, if properly cared for, should enjoy perfect health for the greater part of his life. Nevertheless, he *is* subject to a number of complaints which, if they do arise at all, can very quickly prove fatal, so that it is important for any owner to be able to recognize the first signs of illness in his dog, although it is more than likely that he will keep one for many years without having to put this knowledge to any use. Quite as important as learning what symptoms to look out for is the task of running to earth a really reliable veterinary surgeon, and, above all, one who specializes in dogs; very many practitioners seem to have a knowledge and interest largely restricted to the bigger farm animals, and will bestow their time and attention only very grudgingly upon the smaller fry, an attitude which is, of course, no good to *you*. So do ask the advice of breeders already established in your area before you choose the veterinary surgeon you intend to patronize, and, having made your choice, have his address and telephone number readily available for any emergency and when you do call him in show your confidence in him by supplying him with all the information he requires, accepting his diagnosis rather than attempting to force your own upon him, and finally obeying his instructions implicitly. It is always as well to warn him in advance when you are expecting a bitch to whelp, so that a call in the early hours will not take him by surprise, but try to avoid such calls whenever possible, although he himself will not thank you for delaying to send for him in time when something is obviously wrong. Whenever possible, take your dog to the veterinary surgeon rather than asking him to visit you; this is almost always possible for prophylactic injections and the like, but is not advisable, naturally, if the dog has a high temperature, serious injury, or is suspected of some infectious disease. On the whole, in this matter as in most others connected with dogs, common sense will be your best guide, and should prevent you falling foul of your veterinary surgeon, who should ideally be your best friend in the canine field. When nursing a sick dog you should, of course, be guided by your own veterinary surgeon's views, but warmth is usually the first essential, while Benger's Food and Brand's Essence provide an excellent invalid diet; a raw egg beaten up with sherry is a good pick-me-up. A dry, or even warm nose, incidentally, is not invariably a sign of ill health, and is in any case no reliable guide to the dog's temperature; this should be taken in the anus with an ordinary clinical thermometer ('normal' for a dog is anything from 100·5° to 101·5° F.), but, in the absence of the necessary instrument, a rough and ready assessment may generally be made by placing the hand in the animal's groin, when any excessive heat (or the reverse) is often apparent. A *low* temperature, incidentally, is a more disquieting symptom than a high one.

On the principal that it is better to be safe than sorry, every dog owner is advised to keep by him a special canine medicine chest, as although many of its contents may never be required, if they *are* needed at all they are generally needed in a hurry. The following list contains the bare necessities:

Clinical thermometer
Cotton wool
Bandages
Sharp scissors
Aspirins
Olive oil

Penicillin ointment (obtainable on prescription only)
Thick tape for the improvisation of a muzzle if the patient is obstreperous
Brandy
Glucose

In common with his master, the dog, which is also the most highly domesticated of all animals, seems to have far more ailments 'available' to him now than was the case twenty years ago; this may be due to an actual increase in the number of diseases prevalent, or merely because research has revealed the cause of death in cases where it was previously unknown or put down to some other factor. The following notes cover the ailments most prevalent among Old English Sheepdogs, together with some of their more simple treatments, but makes no pretence to be comprehensive. The Bobtail owner is at least fortunate in that his breed is subject to no specific failing peculiar to itself, such as night-blindness in the Irish Setter, deafness in the Bull Terrier, chronic bronchial disorders in the Bulldog, eczema in the Sealyham, or 'nerves' in the Shetland Sheepdog.

ACCIDENTS

Anybody, human or canine, is liable to be the victim of an accident, and first aid in either case follows similar lines. If you are unfortunate enough to have your dog run over, keep him quiet, move him as little as possible, and send for the veterinary surgeon. Never give any stimulants where haemorrhage is either apparent or suspected internally. If the dog is beside himself with pain, forestall the risk of being severely bitten by muzzling him with a length of tape before attempting to render first aid. Where there is profuse haemorrhage, either due to a road accident, a pad cut by glass, a torn ear, or any other cause, bandage the wound as tightly as possible to stem the bleeding and, where practicable, apply a tourniquet between the wound and the heart; a tourniquet of badage can best be tightened by twisting a pencil or something similar in a loop of the material. Haemorrhage on the tip of an ear or from a wart (melanotic warts on the scrotum are particularly susceptible to this) can often be stopped by the application of a strong paper clip.

BURNS AND SCALDS

Clip away the hair from the affected area and apply any soothing lotion; olive oil, or, indeed, any oily or fatty substance will serve the purpose of allaying the immediate pain, and penicillin ointment will prevent infection of the exposed tissue. Warmth and a drink of milk and glucose will help to allay the shock until the veterinary surgeon arrives.

CANKER

There are two kinds of Canker, the so-called wet and dry. The latter, *otitis externa,* is not really true canker at all, and takes the form of a secretion of brownish powder within the orifice of the ear, which may be cleaned away with the twenty-five per cent calamine and spirit lotion mentioned in Chapter Three. Air should be let into the ear by clipping away all surplus hair. True canker takes the form of an odorous discharge from the ear, the visible parts of which become swollen and inflamed. In its early stages, this may be cured by daily cleansing with a mild solution of antiseptic followed by a dusting of sulphonomide powder, or boracic and zinc oxide, but in its chronic state only an operation (aural resection) will prove effective. This operation is, however, a simple one, and almost invariably a complete success.

COCCIDIOSIS

Until comparatively recently this disease was not known to affect dogs, but is now generally recognized as one of their ailments. Persistent diarrhoea, sometimes streaked with blood and always with a high mucous content, is the only symptom, and the infection is said to remain on the premises where the affected dog has voided faeces for a long period, although I have not myself found this to be the case. A complete cure can be affected under veterinary supervision by a prolonged course of sulpha mezathine taken in conjunction with a special meatless diet composed mainly of milk.

CONSTIPATION

As the faeces of the dog should normally be firm or even hard, this is a condition which rarely arises; should the animal be noticed to have difficulty in voiding faeces, however, or to pass no motions for a few days, a dose of liquid paraffin (about one tablespoonful) will usually be all that is necessary. Castor oil is *not* to be recommended.

COPROPHAGY

Occasional individuals in any breed may suffer from this addiction, which simply means the eating of their own faeces. Some authorities claim that the cause of the trouble is vitamin deficiency, others iron deficiency, but in my experience an increased supply of either seems to have no effect whatsoever, which has led me to believe that this is largely a mental trait, and as such incurable. The careful 'baiting' of faeces with some foul tasting substance, such as turpentine, *might* help, but it is as well to remember that, although coprophagy will certainly not do the animal any *good,* it is equally unlikely to do him a great deal of *harm*, our own revulsion at the practice being mainly connected with our own ethics. All dogs, of course, tend to devour the faeces of herbivores such as goats or horses, which was originally one of the main sources of carbohydrate for the wild dog.

COUGH

While this may be a symptom of some really serious complaint such as distemper or tuberculosis (q.v.), and as such should never be treated lightly, many dogs, like ourselves, have what is no more than a cough in its own rights from time to time, and this will usually yield quite readily to dosing with either olive oil or any proprietary human cough medicine.

DIARRHOEA

Except in the case of coccidiosis, this may well be one of the symptoms of many serious ailments from distemper to jaundice, and should never be treated lightly. Veterinary opinion should usually be sought in such cases, although the trouble may, of course, be no more than the type of stomach upset due to some unsuitable item of diet which is often the cause of similar symptoms in ourselves! I do not advocate the administering of castor oil on the principle that this will clear out the cause of the trouble, as this treatment seems more likely to give additional irritation to an already irritated intestine than to do any real good. (See also Stomach Ailments.)

DISTEMPER COMPLEX

Only a comparatively short time ago the simple distemper of the olden days was considered almost inevitable at some stage or other of a puppy's development, but now that para-distemper, or hard-pad, is upon us it is a very different tale. The initial symptoms of both forms of the disease are the same; inappetance, a slight, dry cough, general malaise, slight temperature, and diarrhoea, becoming persistent, and these are followed by a mucous discharge from the eyes and nose, inflamed eyes, and an expression as though the sufferer had a cracking headache. Perhaps the most terrifying thing of all about this ailment is that the symptoms are so variable, for only one or two of the above may be at first in evidence, the rest following on at intervals of a few days, or all may appear simultaneously. In the case of hard-pad, the actual hardening of the pads very seldom appears, but the nervous symptoms which indicate that the virus has attacked the central nervous system may not arise until the patient is apparently cured or may equally well be the first signs which are noticed. These usually take the form of nervous twitches all over the body, followed by fits and, in extreme cases, a violent pulsating in the head which is clearly visible across the width of a room. The incubation period of the disease is up to three weeks, and its duration may be as long as nine or ten weeks, the virus remaining active on the premises wherever the affected dog has voided faeces or rubbed the mucous from his nose for at least six weeks after the infection has died down. All too often if the victim of hard-pad does not die he is left with permanent nervous disabilities, and, as the onset of the disease is so insidious, veterinary aid is frequently sought when it is too late to effect a cure. Warmth, a nourishing diet containing plenty of raw meat (or cooked if the dog's digestive system is too badly upset to cope with raw), milk, eggs, Benger's Food, and vitamin B, and regular dosing with aspirin will all help the veterinary surgeon's treatment, but the dog must be normal for at least two weeks before he can be considered cured and with no fear of a relapse. Prophylactic treatment is, of course, the answer, and I cannot recommend too strongly that all young stock should be inoculated at about nine weeks of age; in cases where an unimmunized dog is known to have been subjected to infection, a dose of distemper serum will help to tide him over the danger period.

ENTROPION

This, or inverted eyelids, appears to be not uncommon among Bobtails, and should be looked for in all puppies. 'Weepy' eyes are the obvious symptom, and closer examination will reveal that the lids are curled inwards in such a way that the lashes are constantly irritating the eyeball itself. In slight cases drops of liquid paraffin in the eyes may effect a cure, but an operation is usually necessary to put the matter right. The condition appears to be hereditary.

EXTERNAL PARASITES

Although many people would be indignant at the mere suggestion that *their* dogs could possibly be subjected to such infestation, the fact remains that *any* dog, however carefully kept, is liable to pick up fleas, lice, or ticks from some external source at any time. Although many brands of louse powder are on the market, these do not seem to be wholly efficacious unless frequently applied, and that not only on the dog himself, but all over his bedding and anywhere else where he habitually lies down. Bathing in a ten per cent solution of Dettol can be recommended, the dog being immersed for ten minutes in the case of fleas, and five minutes for lice, a repetition being necessary after three days in the latter instance as nothing can destroy the eggs of these parasites, and new infestation will occur as a new batch hatches. It is equally important to deal with the dog's bedding, as fleas habitually leave their host when sated, and will, if necessary, conceal themselves in his bed for many weeks until he returns to give them another meal. Ticks may be killed with paraffin or a cigarette end, and then drawn away with tweezers, care being taken to extract the head.

FLEAS *See external parasites.*

HAEMOTOMA

This is a blood-serum blister, and is a secondary symptom due to the constant scratching caused by some primary irritation, most often canker, q.v. It takes the form of a swelling on the flap of the ear, varying in size from that of a small nut to an area encompassing the whole flap. A veterinary surgeon will tap the fluid, but the primary cause generally requires more attention.

HIP-DISPLASIA

Any prolonged lameness may be found to be due to this cause, which is thought by some to be hereditary. A veterinary surgeon should be consulted, but the cure, if any, is likely to be a difficult business.

INFLUENZA

It is quite possible for the dog to catch this common complaint from his master, and the treatment is the same for both; warmth, a light diet, plenty to drink, and a course of aspirins are usually all that is necessary to restore the sufferer to health.

INTERNAL PARASITES

The most common of these are round and tape worms, and, as most puppies seem to develop some degree of infestation of the former during their early days, routine worming should be undertaken at the age of about six weeks. Should a puppy show serious symptoms of infestation earlier, however, do not hesitate to worm him as early as two or three weeks old. Thinness, voracious or faddy appetite, staring coat or pot-belly may all be symptoms of worm infestation, and round worms may be vomited or noticed in the faeces, where also segments of tapeworm are liable to appear. If the symptoms are present and no worms seen, a specimen of faeces should be sent for analysis as the microscopic hook worm may be present, a parasite which requires veterinary attention. In any case I prefer to obtain worm tablets from my veterinary surgeon rather than rely upon proprietary brands.

LEPTOSPIRAL JAUNDICE

This deadly disease is transmitted through the urine of rats, so dogs living in areas particularly infested with these animals might with advantage be immunized against it. The chief symptoms are inappetance, lethargy, depression, and diarrhoea, with occasional nose-bleeding, and as with distemper, these may well be so slight as to go unnoticed until it is too late. The actual jaundice does not become apparent until a late stage. Injections of serum and antibiotics may save the patient if given in time, and calomel may also be used with good results, but unless the veterinary surgeon is summoned at the onset of the ailment there is very little hope of a cure.

LEPTOSPIRAL NEPHRITIS

This is once more a deadly disease, which in this case attacks and destoys the tissues of the kidneys. Town dogs are more liable to infection than their country cousins, so prophylactic treatment is again invaluable in such cases. A new inoculation giving immunity to both leptospiral jaundice and the distemper complex has recently come onto the market, and this 'two-in-one' injection may go a long way to combating the disease. A high temperature in conjunction with inappetance, constipation, lethargy, an arched back and tucked up loin, pain over the kidneys, and a reduction in urine or difficulty in passing it, with the dog attempting frequent small urinations, are the first symptoms, followed by excessive thirst, red and ulcerated gums, and a strong smell of uraemia on the breath. This was formerly known as Stuttgart's Disease, and often proves fatal, although injections of penicillin are specific if given in time. Needless to say, the veterinary surgeon should be summoned when the first signs are observed.

LICE *See external parasites.*

METRITIS

This is an infection of the uterus brought about by retention of one or part of one placenta after the birth of a litter. In cases where such retention is suspected the veterinary surgeon should be called to administer an injection of pituitrin, followed by a course of penicillin if metritis is already set up. The danger is greater to the litter than the bitch, whose milk may often be poisoned by the toxic matter from the uterus, with dire results to the puppies.

RHEUMATISM

Many dogs are subject to this complaint, and its symptoms can be most alarming if their cause is not known, as the animal may appear to be virtually paralysed if the attack is severe. Fortunately three or four aspirins given three times a day will usually effect an almost miraculous cure.

SLOBBERING

Dogs which suddenly start to dribble excessively should always be examined for the cause, which is most often a fragment of bone stuck between their teeth or across their palates. This can usually be removed without difficulty. Another cause for dribbling, however, may well be bad teeth, when veterinary assistance is called for.

STOMACH AILMENTS

Like his master, the dog periodically suffers from an 'upset tummy', and, assuming that the possibility of this being a symptom of one of the more serious diseases can be ruled out, a day or so of starvation except for light meals of Benger's Food will usually be all that is necessary to put matters right.

TAR

Having such hairy feet, the Bobtail is particularly liable to suffer from tar during hot weather. When the feet are found to be coated with this substance, the hair should be cut away from between the toes and liberal application of lard rubbed well in to soften the deposit prior to washing.

TICKS *See external parasites.*

TUBERCULOSIS

Unfortunately the dog is subject to this disease in all its forms, although it is comparatively rare in incidence. The possibility should not be excluded, however, if the dog has a chronic cough (indicative of T.B. of the lungs), or grows unnaturally thin and, in the final stages, shows a markedly subnormal temperature, when the veterinary surgeon should be consulted, although this ailment is generally considered incurable in dogs.

VOMITING *See stomach ailments.*

WORMS *See internal parasites.*

Although it would be impossible to stress the important part played by your veterinary surgeon if you are to be able to keep any number of dogs with anything approaching confidence, it is only fair to mention that there has recently come into being what *might* prove an invaluable aid to the owner of any type of animal. This is known as radionic therapy (colloquially, 'on the box'), and can alledgedly effect cures of both human and animal patients by remote control, only a blood sample being required for diagnosis and treatment. While I have no personal experience of this method, I know of one elephant and one monkey which recovered after treatment, and one chimpanzee and one tiger which did not—so you can take it or leave it for what it is worth! I shall, however, be glad to supply further details to anybody interested in trying this form of treatment, and this or, indeed, any other queries concerning Old English Sheepdogs, will always find me at the Amberford Kennels, Hill Top house, Ashover, Chesterfield, Derbyshire.

APPENDIX 1

PREFIXES AND KENNELS

AMBERFORD. Mrs. J. A. Keeling, Hill Top House, Ashover, Chesterfield.

BEANVILLE. Miss V. Keeling, The Beeches, Alders Lane, Tansley, Matlock.

BECKINGTON. Mrs. K. Gibson, Coed Fa, Llanbedr, Ruthin, North Wales.

BEWKES. Misses Smailes & Knight Bruce, Bewkes, Newchapel, Lingfield, Surrey.

BLEAKDOWN. Lt-Col. M. D. Lister, Lower Elliotts, Godshill, Isle of Wight.

BLUECOTE. Mr. W. J. Calvey, Catcott, Near Bridgwater, Somerset.

BLUEWAVE. Mrs. E. Rollo, Berry Cottage, Donhead St. Mary, Shaftesbury, Dorset.

BLUMARK. Mr. A. J. Baker, Myrtle House, 171, Cardiff Road, Eastbrook, Dinas-Powis, Glamorgan.

BOBBYCROFT. Miss C. F. Workman, 49, Shipston Road, Stratford-on-Avon.

BOLDWOOD. Mrs. W. Grillet, 32, Panton Street, Cambridge.

BROADWELL. Mr. J. Wasley, Hill Crest, Broadford, Near Coleford, Gloucestershire.

CEMAES. Mrs. J.D.James, 1, Albert Road, Cheltenham, Gloucestershire.

DALCROY. Miss A. Lloyd, Old Rectory, Hammerwich, Near Lichfield.

DANUM KENNELS. Mr. F. Brocklesby, 85a, Bentley Road, Doncaster.

DAPHNIS. Mr. E.J. J. Minnett, Riverdale, Tixall, Stafford.

DUROYA. Mrs. A. E. Woodiwiss, Hillfarm, Unstone, Near Sheffield.

ELLINGHURST. Mrs. J. C. R. Chapman, Ellinghurst Farm, Pilning, Near Bristol.

FAIRACRES. Mrs. E. M. Bloor, Fairacres Kennels, Lilleshall, Shropshire.

FARLEYDENE. Mr. G. Gooch, Wraxall, Lower Road, East Farleigh, Kent.

FERNVILLE. Mr. N. W. R. Harrison, 25, High Street, Swallownest, Near Sheffield.

GORDALE. Mr. C. C. St. J. Stacey, Gordale Kennels, Frome, Somerset.

GRENDONFELL. Mrs. I. F. Cooke, 12, Fairview, Horsham, Sussex, and Mr. A. E. Mason, 106, Lowbrook Lane, Solihull, Warwickshire.

GREYSTOKE. Miss J. M. Back, 26, Old Kirk Road, Corstorphine, Edinburgh.

HORNASH. Mr. & Mrs. R. F. Mathews, Hornash Farm, Shadoxhurst, Near Ashford, Kent.

KEANDOR. Mr. & Mrs. A. R. Wood, The Homestead, Thurnscoe Road, Bolton-on-Dearne, Near Rotherham.

KNOCKANYLN. Mr. J. A. Muirhead, Cromdale, Bridge of Weir, Renfrewshire.

LANSEER. Mr. & Mrs. W. Ashley, Garden Flat, 7, Highbury Grove, London N.5.

LINNIFOLD. Mr. & Mrs. J. S. Mason, Corfe, Taunton, Somerset.

LITTLEPARC KENNELS. Mrs. E. Jackson, Littleparc, Thornhill, Llanishen, Cardiff.

MARLAY. Mrs. H. Booth, Birches Brow, Aughton, Near Ormskirk, Lancashire.

PASTELBLUE. Miss I. Webster, Ivy House Lane, Hastings.

PEARLSTONE. Miss P. M. Peart, Dunn Hill House, Hungerford, Berkshire.

PINEHURST. Mrs. W. Heyward, Pinehurst Kennels, Jarvis Brook, Sussex.

RECULVER. Mr. & Mrs. A. G. Wilkinson, 27, Beaconsfield Road, Hastings.

ROLLINGSEA. Mrs. J. R. Gould, 135, Mount Wise, Newquay, Cornwall.

SHEPTON. Miss F. Tilley, East Compton House, Shepton Mallet.

SQUAREFOUR. Mrs. I. C. Nicol, Woodlands, Romano Bridge, West Linton, Peeblesshire.

TALMORA. Mrs. S. M. Talbot, Collier Street, Marden, Tonbridge, Kent.

TANSLEY. Mrs. E. Goodwin, Cunnery Farm, Tansley, Matlock.

WATCHERS. Miss Tucker, North Heath Barn, Pulborough, Sussex.

WEIRWOOD. Mrs. C. Barclay, Wyldewoods, Woodgreen Road, Waltham Abbey, Essex.

YASABEL. Mrs. M. Murray, 27, Marnham Crescent, Greenford, Middlesex.

YELDHAMS. Mr. & Mrs. H. Linsell-Clark, Yeldhams Farm, Finchingfield, Near Braintree, Essex.

APPENDIX 2

OLD ENGLISH SHEEPDOG CLUBS

NORTH-WESTERN OLD ENGLISH SHEEPDOG CLUB Founded 1923
Secretary: Mrs. Woodiwiss, Hillfarm, Unstone, Near Sheffield.

OLD ENGLISH SHEEPDOG CLUB Founded 1888
Secretary: Mrs. I. R. Lapwood, 810, Kenton Lane, Harrow Weald, Middlesex.

OLD ENGLISH SHEEPDOG CLUB OF SCOTLAND
Secretary: Mr. & Mrs. J. Nicol, Woodlands, Romano Bridge, West Linton, Peeblesshire.

SOUTH-EASTERN OLD ENGLISH SHEEPDOG CLUB
Secretary: Mr. A. A. G. Akehurst, 19, Waldenhurst Road, Saint Mary Cray, Kent.

* * *

The address of the Kennel Club is 1–4, Clarges Street, Piccadilly, London, W.1., and all communications should be addressed to the Secretary.

GLOSSARY

Amble: The characteristic gait of the Old English Sheepdog, the main feature being the 'sailor's roll' of the hindaction.

Break: Term applied to the slight wave of the Sheepdog's coat.

Brisket: The area of the ribs immediately behind the shoulders

Butterfly nose: All puppies are born with pink noses, which go black in spots at first; the term is applicable to this stage, which is sometimes permanent.

Challenge Certificate: At Championship Shows a Challenge Certificate is offered for dogs and bitches, and is awarded to the best of each sex. Three such Certificates, gained under different judges, earn the animal the title of Champion.

Cowhocks: A condition of the hind legs when these come close together at the 'elbows'.

Cynologist: One who makes a study of dogs.

Docking: The amputation of a puppy's tail.

Feathering: The dense hair standing out from the fore-legs.

Foetus: The unborn young.

Foetal Membrane: The amnion, or sac, in which the foetus develops.

Gestation Period: The time elapsing between mating and the birth of the young.

Ham: Thigh or femur.

Hock: 'Elbow' on the hind leg.

Loin: Area of the back immediately above the pelvic girdle, or hip joints.

Mammary Glands: Udders or breasts.

Oestrus: Heat or season, when ripe ova descend from the ovaries in readiness for mating.

Ova: Eggs.

Overshot: A condition wherein the upper jaw protrudes markedly beyond the lower.

Parturition: Giving birth.

Pigmentation: Colouration, usually applied to dark eyes, nose, lips, etc., rather than coat colour.

Placenta: The afterbirth, attached to the wall of the uterus during pregnancy to draw nutriment from the bloodstream of the dam for her unborn young.

Prophylactic: Preventative; applied to inoculation and immunization.

Season: See oestrus.

Stop: The point at which the forehead rises from the nose.

Umbilicus: The navel.

Umbilical cord: A 'string' of vein and artery connecting the placenta to the foetus, via the umbilicus.

Undershot: A condition wherein the lower jaw protrudes markedly beyond the upper.

Uterus: Womb.

Vagina: Passage leading to the uterus.

Wall-eyed: A condition wherein the dog has eyes of different colours, usually brown and china blue. (See page 18.)

BIBLIOGRAPHY

Gwynne-Jones, Olwen. *Modern Kennel Management.*
Gwynne-Jones, Olwen. *The popular Guide to Puppy Rearing.*
Tilley, Henry Arthur. *The Old English Sheepdog.*

INDEX